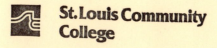

Chalcatzingo

NEW ASPECTS OF ANTIQUITY

General Editor: COLIN RENFREW

Consulting Editor for the Americas: JEREMY A. SABLOFF

DAVID C. GROVE

Chalcatzingo

Excavations on the Olmec Frontier

with 141 illustrations, 15 in color

THAMES AND HUDSON

First published in the USA in 1984 by Thames and Hudson Inc., 500 Fifth Avenue, New York, New York 10110

Library of Congress Catalog Card Number 83-51427

Printed and bound in Hungary

Contents

General Editor's foreword

There are no more fascinating and mysterious people in the world of archaeology today than the Olmec. Precursors of the great civilizations of Central America, they are known from sites which lie not in central Mexico, scene of many later developments in Mexican history, but down in the hot and humid tropical forests bordering the Gulf of Mexico, over 200 miles to the east. The story of their discovery and investigation impinges upon the whole intensive and dynamic development of archaeological research in Meso-america in recent years, itself one of the hotspots of current progress in world archaeology.

The fascination with the Olmec is not simply a romantic one, although the uncovering of huge stone heads in the tropical forests, or of precious jade artifacts in the form of so-called 'werejaguars' is dramatic enough. It is rather that here, perhaps for the first time in the Americas, we see the beginnings of a society so centralized and so highly organized that in its later stages it may be dignified by the name 'the state.' We are studying, then, that process of social elaboration and development seen elsewhere in the world which is of inescapable significance for us all: the progress towards civilization.

At first sight it is unexpected that a site located in central Mexico, so far from the Gulf coast, should be one of the most interesting and relevant for our understanding of the Olmec. But so it is. Chalcatzingo, whose excavation plays the central role in the story of discovery and research in this book, lies in the Mexican state of Morelos, separated by a modest range of mountains from the Valley of Mexico to the north. Here, in 1932, remarkable rock carvings were discovered whose style unmistakably resembles the art of the Olmec heartland down on the Gulf. Why this should be so, and how to explain the other indications of Olmec 'influence' in central Mexico at what turns out to be a remarkably early date, are questions which Professor Grove set out to answer by fieldwork over several years. His answers are given here.

In the course of the work, remains of what were clearly public buildings of considerable scale were unearthed, and several important relief carvings discovered. It was possible to piece together a very clear picture of the life of the inhabitants, as well as to make inferences about the social organization of their society. It is the solution to Professor Grove's initial questions about the

Olmec lowlands, however, which gives his account its much wider relevance. In developing the idea of an Olmec 'frontier,' of a system of alliances perhaps promoted by marriages between local chiefs and the families of Olmec rulers down on the Gulf, he offers one solution to a problem which increasingly concerns archaeologists in many parts of the world. Again and again we find evidence for the spread of ideas, and for the development of areas of considerable uniformity of culture, without always being able to understand what caused these things. The old notions of 'migrations of peoples' often turn out to be inappropriate – as in this case – and to speak of the 'diffusion' of culture does not in itself help at all. What we are seeking is some understanding of the mechanisms, in clear human terms, which underlay these interactions. The work on Chalcatzingo offers one approach which will be widely studied.

David Grove writes with the firm commitment of the real field archaeologist. Indeed one of the pleasures of this book comes from the overview which it gives of the archaeologist out on location. For here is history being written, in an area which earlier was archaeologically unknown, about people long forgotten, who left no written records and whose important center at Chalcatzingo faded away shortly after 500 BC! Despite these formidable limitations the result is a very clear one. Various techniques of the archaeologist are here deployed to reconstruct the prehistory of the site. And the work doesn't stop at that. The data are used to answer the much broader questions about the Olmec, and indeed about culture process in general, which originally stimulated the research. This is a graphic account of the modern archaeologist at work – both as digger and as thinker.

Colin Renfrew

Consulting Editor's foreword

Archaeology has undergone a series of major changes in recent years. Often labeled 'the new archaeology' in the professional literature, these changes have had a significant impact on how archaeologists plan research, how they conduct fieldwork, and how they analyze and interpret the data they collect. Yet, to date, few of these new ideas have been communicated to the interested public, most of whom remain unsure of the wide variety of fresh trends in archaeological thinking.

The impression is sometimes given that the principal advances in the past couple of decades have been in the realms of field technique and laboratory analysis. Most amateurs and students – if not laymen generally – are sufficiently knowledgeable to reject the longstanding, *Raiders of the Lost Ark* image of archaeologists as pith-helmeted adventurers searching for lost cities and gold statues. But the more recent view that modern archaeologists are white-smocked scientists applying ultramodern laboratory techniques and using sophisticated nuclear hardware to bring the past to life is also an inaccurate one. Even though the development of new analytical techniques has been significant, the most important shift in archaeology today is in disciplinary goals and methodology. It is sad to report that little of this has filtered through to the general reader.

Many archaeologists seem reluctant to present their procedures as well as their findings in a form intelligible to a wide audience. Instead they conjure up a 'black box,' describing how they start out with certain objectives, undertake a series of complex research procedures which are too difficult to explain, and then obtain results which they *are* happy to discuss in great detail. The public is left with the impression that more fieldwork automatically produces more and better results. Professional archaeologists should face the challenge of explaining modern methodology clearly and with the minimum of jargon. It is the responsibility of the whole discipline, not just a few scholars who enjoy writing for non-professional audiences.

It is to Professor Grove's lasting credit that he has not shirked that responsibility. One of the greatest strengths of *Chalcatzingo* is the author's willingness and ability to walk the reader through the various stages of research, with particular emphasis on the planning and execution of fieldwork and on how interpretations are arrived at. Professor Grove's clearly written, well-organized discussion is essential reading not only for those interested in the Olmec and in Mesoamerican prehistory, but for all those fascinated by the rise of ancient civilizations, and the development of archaeology in general.

Jeremy A. Sabloff

Preface

The archaeological research at Chalcatzingo owes its success to many people. From the very beginning the investigations were a joint effort of US and Mexican archaeologists. I planned and directed the project from start to finish, but could not have done so without the able assistance of Mexican archaeologist Jorge Angulo who served as my co-director for the first field season, and archaeologist Raul Arana, the co-director for the second and third seasons. The laboratory work in Mexico and particularly the difficult task of pottery analysis was under the capable supervision of Ann Cyphers Guillen. Archaeology students from Mexican and US universities supervised the individual excavation areas, participated in the regional surface-reconnaissance, and assisted in the laboratory analyses. Three doctoral dissertations and several masters theses have so far resulted from the research. A scientific publication providing detailed documentation of the excavations and artifacts is being published through the University of Texas Press.

The major funding for the Chalcatzingo project came from the National Science Foundation of the United States. Additional grants, including those for a photogrammetric site map, were provided by the National Geographic Society of Washington, DC. Supplementary support also came from the National Institute of Anthropology and History (INAH) in Mexico, the Research Board of the University of Illinois, and from a private donor.[1]

The data used in the book are the result of the hard work of each and every project participant, not the least of whom were the people of Chalcatzingo. They became skilled workers and close friends, and are justifiably proud of their rich heritage. My colleagues and I have spent long hours analyzing and discussing the data. Many of the interpretations given here resulted from those discussions, some have been drawn from ideas presented in chapters which my colleagues and I have written for the detailed and lengthy excavation report,[2] and others are my own hypotheses. However, my colleagues should not be held responsible for errors or disagreements, those belong to me.

Visitors to Chalcatzingo will find that the official guidebook, written by project co-director Jorge Angulo, uses a greatly different numbering system from the one I use in the following pages.[3] His provides a complete revision of the long-established sequential numbering system based on order of discovery, and it innovates by separating each monument group and numbering within that group. In the text I discuss the monument groups separately, but I have retained the sequential system, with only minor revisions, and have added carvings discovered by our project. Only time will tell which system will gain continued acceptance.

1 The archaeological culture called Olmec

The hot and humid coastal plains of the southern Gulf of Mexico, in the Mexican states of Tabasco and southern Veracruz, are covered by a thick deciduous tropical forest which is occasionally broken by areas of savannah. *fig. 1* Much of this low plain floods during the annual rainy season which begins in June and continues into December. Until recently, when modern roads cut across the region, boats were the most appropriate form of transportation, particularly during the rainy period. At first glance the coastal plain seems an unlikely habitat for the development of one of ancient Mesoamerica's first complex cultures, the Olmec. Yet archaeologists actively investigating Olmec prehistory not only view this swampy tropical zone as the heartland of this ancient people, but also interpret recent archaeological discoveries there as indicating that the elaborate Olmec development was indigenous, and not intrusive from another region, as some scholars had once hypothesized.

Olmec culture flourished on the Gulf coast during the period approximately 1200–500 BC, the period archaeologists call the Preclassic or Formative. Because of their elaborate monumental art, fine jade, and other exotic artifacts, writers dealing with the Olmec have tended to indulge in superlatives, for this people indeed seems precocious at that period of Mesoamerican prehistory. The Olmec are usually credited with originating Mesoamerica's first great art style, its first major religion, its complex calendar systems, and many other features important to the region's later civilizations. For that reason some scholars have considered them to be the 'mother culture' of those civilizations, and one archaeologist, Michael Coe, has even called them 'America's first civilization.'[4] Some of those superlatives may be well deserved, but others should be viewed with extreme caution. Recent archaeological research in Belize, Oaxaca, and other areas, has disclosed contemporary cultures which were developing independently and equally elaborately in their own ways. The great civilizations of the Maya, Teotihuacan, and the Zapotecs have multiple ancestral roots, only one of which belongs to the Gulf coast Olmec. But the Olmec achievement for its time and place was certainly spectacular.

The first discovery of an Olmec monument, in the 1860s, was so unusual that it has become a legend. A farmer in southern Veracruz, clearing away the dense tropical vegetation to open new land for a sugar plantation, noticed a large rounded object protruding from the forest floor. Thinking it to be the base of a large overturned iron caldron, he reported the find to his foreman, and workers were brought over to unearth it. What they had thought was a caldron base turned out to be the top of a colossal human head, magnificently carved from dark volcanic stone. The head stood nearly 1.5 m tall, and the heavy facial features were beautifully executed. The place of that discovery is the archaeological site today known as Tres Zapotes.

As time passed, other stone carvings were found in the region, some of which showed humans with baby-like and even feline-like facial characteristics. Jade objects also began appearing in collections from the area, and occasionally those also were engraved with the same unusual human faces. Because ethnohistorical documents spoke of *Olmeca*, 'people of the rubber country,' who had inhabited the Gulf coast region several centuries before the arrival of the Spanish in 1519, the various carvings and artifacts were attributed to them. Much later, when it was realized that the makers of such objects had lived nearly 2000 years before the *Olmeca* mentioned in the documents, the name Olmec was already in standard use by archaeologists. Some researchers have attempted to introduce other names, but the term Olmec persists. In order to avoid confusion, the later, proto-historic, group is now usually referred to by scholars as the *Olmeca-Xicallanca*.

The splendor of Gulf coast Olmec culture first came to general public attention through the writings of the late Matthew Stirling, whose explorations along the Gulf coast were documented by *National Geographic Magazine* under titles such as 'Great Stone Faces of the Mexican Jungle,' 'Finding Jewels of Jade in a Mexican Swamp,' and 'La Venta's Green Stone Tigers.'[5] This was pioneering research, and Stirling, who most of us consider to have been the 'father of Olmec archaeology,' carried out investigations at three of the four major Olmec centers known, La Venta, San Lorenzo, and

plate 78 Tres Zapotes. Since that time only La Venta and San Lorenzo have received further serious scholarly attention. The fourth center, Laguna de los Cerros, has only been test-excavated.

The ecological setting of the four centers is riverine. Each is situated inland from the coast on hills or other high ground which places them above the annual flooding of the coastal plain. In antiquity, during both the rainy and dry seasons, the river systems of the Gulf coast must have functioned as the principal routes of communication and commerce in the region. The rivers also played a key role in the development and maintenance of the Olmec in this swampy tropical setting. The annual floods which sweep down from the hills left rich levee deposits next to the rivers, and when the water receded the fertile alluvium could be planted with a variety of crops including maize, beans, and squash, the staples of the Mesoamerican diet. At the same time, the rivers and the ox-bow lakes produced by their remnant meanders became a lucrative source of fish protein. For that reason, Michael Coe and Richard Diehl have labeled the Olmec as 'The People of the River.'[6]

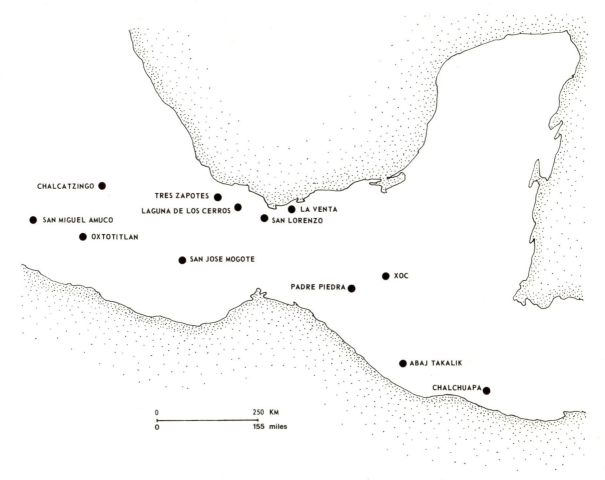

CHALCATZINGO ●

TRES ZAPOTES ●
LAGUNA DE LOS CERROS ●
SAN MIGUEL AMUCO ●
OXTOTITLAN ●
● LA VENTA
● SAN LORENZO

SAN JOSE MOGOTE ●

● XOC
PADRE PIEDRA ●

● ABAJ TAKALIK
CHALCHUAPA ●

0   250 KM
0   155 miles

1 Map of Mesoamerica showing the Gulf coast centers, Chalcatzingo, and other Formative period sites mentioned in the book.

The region's ecology is not completely homogeneous, since it changes as one moves from east to west. La Venta and San Lorenzo, which may have been the two largest centers, are in the east. Tres Zapotes and Laguna de los Cerros, in the west, are both located near the Tuxtla mountains, a low range of volcanic hills which provided a source of basalt for the many monuments carved at the centers, as well as for important domestic tools such as those for grinding corn. Some of the cindercone volcanos of the Tuxtla mountains may likewise have inspired the shape of La Venta's main pyramid mound (see chapter 9).

Although archaeological attention has focused on major Olmec centers, and there have been no intensive surveys designed to locate smaller sites, it is possible to use the present data to postulate at least a three-level hierarchy of Olmec settlements: firstly, major centers; next, a few dependent secondary ones; and lastly, numerous small villages and hamlets. A major center such as La Venta can be considered 'primary' in the hierarchy because of its size, its numerous earthen mounds, and its many stone monuments glorifying particular rulers. Secondary centers seem to be those archaeological sites with only one or two monuments and a few major mounds, while villages lower in the hierarchy lack monumental art and architecture and can probably be located only by the remains of refuse deposits.

Although mentioned here and by other archaeologists as a major center, the importance of Tres Zapotes may have been overestimated for the Olmec period. The site has five separate mound groups, most of which may post-date the Olmec settlement. Further, only a few Olmec period monuments have been recovered there. It will take additional research to determine if Tres Zapotes had indeed been a primary center or merely a secondary one aligned with Laguna de los Cerros.

Whatever its size and role during the period of Olmec culture, Tres Zapotes became important after the Olmec decline about 500 BC, as witnessed by its carved monuments. Stela C, discovered at the site by Matthew Stirling, was carved by post-Olmec people with one of the oldest calendric inscriptions known in Mesoamerica: a so-called 'long count' date of 7.16.6.16.18 (31 BC in the most commonly accepted correlation system). Interestingly, it is the presence of this early long count date at a site with important Olmec roots that has led some researchers to hypothesize that Mesoamerica's complex calendar systems originated with the Olmec. Early long count dates are also found on monuments at sites on the Pacific coast of southern Mesoamerica, and it is premature to credit the Olmec with originating complex calendrics since no such carvings appear upon any known Olmec monuments.

Lack of sufficient archaeological data from Gulf coast Olmec sites has long plagued archaeologists attempting to understand this culture. The problem has been compounded by the fact that Olmec-like ceramic vessels, clay figurines, fine jade ornaments, and even stone carvings have been found in other areas of Mesoamerica including central Mexico, southern Mexico and Guatemala, and parts of Central America. At Gulf coast centers we know that Olmec 'art' is executed in three major media: ceramics (vessels and figurines), jade and other fine green stone (jewelry, celts, figurines), and stone (a variety of plates VII–IX, XV statues, stelae, colossal heads, and massive rectangular 'altars'). The first two categories are made up of smaller objects which apparently had ritual and/or plates XI, 70 status value. Figurines frequently have baby-like facial features, and similar babyfaces appear on humans in carvings or engraved in jade. At times various supernatural elements such as serrated eyebrows or fangs are added to the faces. This frequently creates a feline-like aspect to the face and these plates 66–7 depictions have been labeled 'werejaguars' – a creature partly human and partly jaguar. Both baby-like and 'werejaguar' figures appear on some monumental art, but the major theme in that medium seems to be dedicated to rulership (see also chapters 5 and 9). The presence of these Olmec-like ceramics, jades, and occasional rock carvings outside the heartland has created the so-called Olmec problem, and has led to a great number of attempts to explain their presence at those other sites.

The 'problem' stems from many factors, not the least of which is the fact that although several scholars attempted to define the 'Olmec style,' such definitions were often vague, for there was little information from the Gulf coast centers themselves to aid in their construction. The scarcity of heartland data has resulted in an 'Olmec style' to some extent defined by objects and art found at non-Gulf coast sites, and for one or another reason identified and accepted as 'Olmec.' It is only *assumed* that such objects or motifs are to be found as well at Gulf coast Olmec sites and to have been significant there. This situation has led to circular reasoning in the literature, for how better to 'prove' Olmec origins outside the heartland than to define 'Olmec' by traits which occur at sites outside the Gulf coast? Some or many of the objects and motifs used to identify 'Olmec' and also found elsewhere may well be part of a common set of religious symbolism shared by several early societies in southern Mesoamerica around 1000 BC, including the Gulf coast Olmec, who simply displayed that set of iconography to a far greater degree than others and who included it on a medium not shared by those other societies, monumental art. It must also be remembered that as societies evolved, so also did their pottery, their monuments, and their art. The so-called Olmec style was not static but changed over time, a fact that many studies on the Olmec have failed to consider. Some of these changes will be discussed in later chapters.

Perhaps the greatest quantity of Olmec-style artifacts and art outside the heartland has come from archaeological sites in highland central Mexico, and particularly the states of Mexico, Puebla, Morelos, and Guerrero. Most are the small portable items, such as babyface figures in clay, ceramic bowls decorated with 'werejaguar' motifs, and jade artifacts which on occasion are carved with baby or feline-like visages. But in addition, one central-Mexican archaeological site has a number of elaborate rock carvings executed in a style closely resembling the carved art of the Gulf coast centers. This book deals with that site, Chalcatzingo.

plates 69, 71

In the next chapter, Chalcatzingo is placed in its central Mexican context and a brief introduction to that region's prehistory is presented. Chapter 4 discusses the site's growth and decline in relationship to its immediate area as well as to the central Mexican region. The major chronological periods (phases) used in presenting the data are those which were worked out in the field and in the lab through an analysis of the ceramic stratigraphy. The phases are named for places or things of local importance: *amate*, the common name for a species of wild fig tree; *barranca*, the steep-sided gorge of the Amatzinac River; and *cantera*, a common name for the rock from the mountain cliffs when used for building material.

The subsequent chapters deal with the ancient village of Chalcatzingo, the life of its inhabitants, and the meaning of its monuments. Only after that is the

Gulf coast dealt with for comparative purposes, and hypotheses presented to account for Chalcatzingo's Olmec qualities. Throughout the book I have attempted not to overemphasize the Gulf coast features, for in large measure the site's artifacts are central Mexican. At the same time it must be admitted that it is those very Gulf coast traits which made Chalcatzingo unique among its highland neighbors and conferred upon it a special status.

2 Chalcatzingo and its environment

In sharp contrast to the flatness of the tropical coastal plains characteristic of major Olmec centers such as San Lorenzo and La Venta, central Mexico can be likened topographically to a crumpled paper tossed upon a map. Rugged mountains cross the country from the Pacific Ocean eastward to the coastal plains which fringe the Gulf of Mexico. Within the mountains are broad valleys with rich alluvial soils, and a temperate climate well suited to maize agriculture.

The focal point of the highlands today is the Basin of Mexico. This large *fig. 2* valley, at an altitude of over 2200 m, is the location of Mexico City, a metropolis of twelve million people, built upon the ruins of the Aztec capital of Tenochtitlan. The large lake once contained by the Basin was drained by the Spanish and its bed is now largely covered by Mexico City's urban sprawl. Gone too are the vestiges of ancient settlements which ringed the lake's shores.

To the south, separated from the Basin by the Ajusco mountain range, is the state of Morelos. That region, with elevations closer to 1300 m, has a warmer, subtropical climate. For centuries, residents of the Basin have traveled to Morelos to escape the chill. Even the Aztec emperor Montezuma periodically sought its warmth. The Aztec cities of the Basin likewise coveted the agricultural richness of Morelos and gained access through conquest.

Much of Morelos is characterized by broad humid river plains. Today this area is often hidden beneath sugar cane, a crop introduced by the Spanish. However, the natural humidity beneficial for cane growing made these same lands attractive 3000 years earlier to pre-irrigation agriculturists. Remains of their villages lie obscured beneath the dense fields of cane.

Eastern Morelos is an exception, being far more arid. There a flat plain stretches south from the volcano Popocatepetl, whose 5750-m cone-shaped peak marks the eastern end of the Ajusco mountain range and the northeast corner of Morelos state. Cutting sharply and deeply into the soft volcanic soils at the foot of Popocatepetl is the Amatzinac River which runs south along that *plate 1* eastern plain. Because the river has cut itself a deep *barranca* (or gorge), it provides only limited natural humidity to the valley and offers little easy access to its waters. For that reason, the valley of the Amatzinac River lacks the agricultural potential of areas to the west or east, and that, together with the *fig. 3*

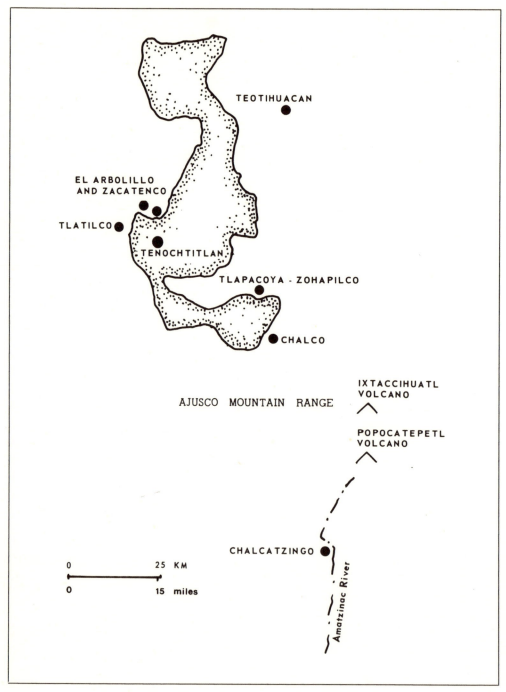

2 *Central Mexico, with the location of sites mentioned in the text.*

scarcity of surface water, was a limiting factor to ancient settlement and population growth.

Dominating the flat and otherwise nearly featureless valley floor are the remnants of three ancient igneous intrusions, a type of mountain known to geologists as an *inselberg* ('island mountain') because it looks like an island rising above the surrounding landscape.[7] Each *inselberg*, with its stark rock cliffs, stands over 300 m above the valley floor, and serves as a landmark visible from great distances.

The northernmost rock massif is the Cerro Jantetelco (*cerro* is Spanish for hill). This mountain matches the description and location of a sacred mountain shrine, *Teocuicani*, described by Aztecs to the 16th-century Dominican friar Diego Durán.[8] About 4 miles south is the long, loaf-shaped Cerro Gordo, and between those mountains is the central intrusion marked by the paired hills which rise above the archaeological site of Chalcatzingo – the Cerro Delgado and the Cerro Chalcatzingo. On the terraced hillside at the base of these peaks lay a settlement which by 700 BC was unique in central Mexico: only there have archaeologists found early monumental architecture and elaborate bas-relief carvings.

plate 2
plate 5

The name Chalcatzingo is from the *Nahuatl* language, a tongue spoken by the Aztecs of the Basin of Mexico, and by the Tlalhuica, the indigenous inhabitants of Morelos at the time of the Spanish conquest in the early 16th century. It has been claimed that in the 14th and 15th centuries, towns in Morelos conquered by Basin of Mexico cities were renamed after the conquering city, with the addition of a diminutive '-zingo' suffix to indicate a subordinate or tributary status. Thus the town of Xochimilcatzingo in central Morelos may have been conquered by Xochimilco (known to tourists today for its floating gardens) and Chalcatzingo by Chalco. That latter city, in the southeastern Basin of Mexico, was the nearest Basin city to the Amatzinac valley. If this is so, the translation of Chalcatzingo could be taken to mean 'Little place of the people of Chalco.'

Although we know that Xochimilco and Chalco did conquer areas of Morelos, only a few Morelos towns carry '-zingo' endings. The archaeological evidence does not disclose any special relationship between these particular sites and their supposed Basin of Mexico conquerors, and I am inclined to believe that the translations do not carry a meaning of conquest. I favor an alternative translation which seems more in line with Chalcatzingo's early importance and with our discovery that at least one bas-relief carving had been the subject of special religious attention a few hundred years prior to the Spanish conquest.

The '-zingo' suffix is not simply a diminutive, but one which expresses sacredness or reverence. In this case the name could be translated as 'the revered place of the people of Chalco.' However, the name Chalco itself may have a particular significance. It derives from the *Nahuatl* word for green stone or jade – *chalchihuitl* – a term synonymous with the 'precious' water

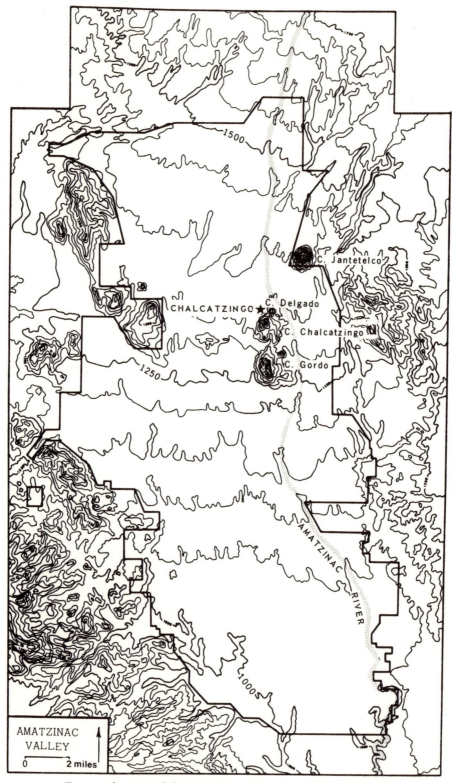

3 *Topographic map of the Amatzinac valley (contour lines in meters).*

symbolized by jade. Chalcatzingo may well mean 'the revered place of sacred water.' The appropriateness of this translation will become apparent in the discussion of the site's best-known bas-relief carving, Monument 1 (see chapter 8).

The modern village of Chalcatzingo, which lends its name to the archaeological zone, is situated about 1 mile north of the site, near the *barranca* (gorge) of the Amatzinac River. It is located at one of the few points *plate 3* where the normally sheer-sided *barranca* momentarily opens, permitting access to the river and easy crossing to the other side. The people of Chalcatzingo are primarily farmers, who spoke *Nahuatl* up to the 19th century, but now only Spanish.

The town is typical of rural central Mexico. A small plaza with a bandstand and basketball court is the focal point of village life. The bandstand, part of a 'modernization' effort by the state government, goes virtually unused, for the town has no band. The basketball court on the other hand is well used, and the village team has won several championships in the valley. To the east of the plaza is a large churchyard with a small, quaint Catholic church, parts of which were constructed during the 16th century. Two other old churches, now abandoned, stand within a few blocks of the plaza.

Most houses in the village are large, relatively simple one- or two-room structures constructed from handmade sunbaked *adobe* (clay) bricks. Their façades are often plastered. Materials used to roof them range from grass thatch to modern corrugated asbestos sheets. A striking feature of most house lots is the *cuexcomate* granary used for storing corn. These granaries, made of *plate 5* clay covering a frame of cane and wood, look like huge inverted bottles with thatched roofs. *Cuexcomate* granaries were once distributed in a band running eastward from Morelos to the state of Veracruz. Today Chalcatzingo is one of the few places where they can still be found, and even there the construction of *cuexcomates* is a dying art.

The farmers of Chalcatzingo still cultivate their fields using wooden ploughs drawn by oxen. Maize is the major subsistence crop grown, while squash, beans, tomatoes, and peanuts are important secondary ones. In recent years some villagers have turned from subsistence to cash-crop farming, growing tomatoes and watermelons for sale commercially. Most farmers, however, still cling to the crops which have been traditional for several millennia. Modern corn hybrids, fertilizers, and insecticides are usually shunned due to prohibitive costs.

The archaeological zone, to the southeast of the village, is in a natural amphitheater formed between the Cerro Chalcatzingo and the Cerro Delgado. About 1000 BC, several hundred years after the first inhabitants had settled on the hillside, the western slopes of the amphitheater area were reworked to create a series of long, broad terraces. The major configuration is essentially *fig. 4, plate 5* three large steps, over 300 m long and up to 100 m wide, leading from the flat valley floor to the boulder-covered talus slopes along the base of the two

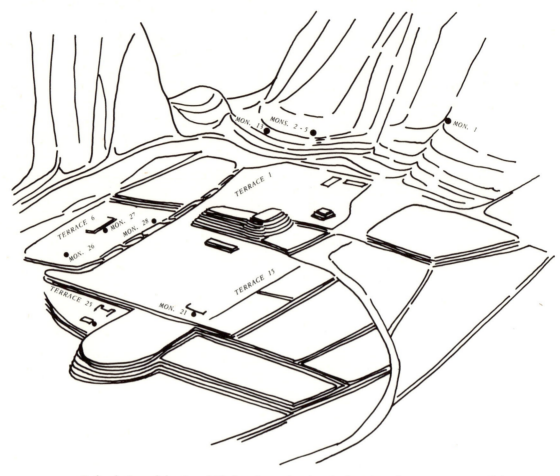

4 *Stylized view of the site of Chalcatzingo, showing the location of major terraces and monuments (compare with fig. 9).*

mountains. Ancient as well as recent alterations have subdivided the terracing into a series of smaller fields, which remain the basic units farmed today by the villagers of Chalcatzingo. Although that land is only about a quarter of the town's communal holdings, the farmers regard it as the best of all.

The terraces are unirrigated, for the only immediate water source is a small spring on the flatlands directly below the terraces. The spring's output is very limited today but is still used to irrigate a small strip of land along its watercourse which runs to the *barranca* of the river. It is possible that a similar form of simple gravity irrigation was used by the site's prehistoric inhabitants. The spring would also have been their nearest and easiest source of drinking water.

It is no exaggeration to say that the fields at Chalcatzingo are rocky: an Irish farmer might feel right at home there. The stones, both large and small, have fallen from the cliffs which hover over the site, while many were brought up from the riverbed in the distant past to use in construction. For several hundred years the rocks have interfered with the farmer's wooden ploughs. Small rocks were ignored or thrown to the field borders. Large stones, more difficult to move, were reburied deeper, beneath the reach of the plough. Sometimes those larger ones were actually broken monuments with bas-relief carving. On a few occasions, however, farmers found carvings and removed them to the village where they were either kept by the finder or displayed on the plaza. One such carving sits there today, but the others have disappeared.

Stone from the cliffs and terraces has been used for several centuries as building material. The village churches, house foundations, and much of the nearby ex-hacienda Santa Clara were constructed from rock 'mined' from the site. There is evidence that some rocks of archaeological significance were dynamited to break them up for building material, and some monuments may have suffered a similar fate.

Chalcatzingo's fame came with the discovery of its Olmec-style rock carvings, executed on the natural cliff face of the Cerro Chalcatzingo and on very large boulders lying on the talus slopes below the sheer cliffs. For centuries the village children cutting firewood or tending animals on the mountain slopes, and the farmers planting the terraced fields, must have been aware of many of the carvings. However, the villagers did not consider them significant and they went unreported. It is therefore interesting that in 1932 the carvings were 'discovered' through the accidental exposure of a large bas-relief high on the Cerro Chalcatzingo.

The find came at a time of awakening national interest in Mexico's rich prehispanic heritage, when mass communication was beginning to bring rural Mexico into touch with developments throughout the country. The newly found carving was now seen as significant, and news of it spread beyond the village. The tale of its discovery survives in several versions. The gist is as follows:

One night in 1932 a tremendous storm came. The wind blew, rain fell in torrents, and trees toppled on the mountainside. During the height of the downpour a rain serpent came over the top of the Cerro Chalcatzingo and down the hillside. It washed earth from the hillside and flooded the fields below with water. When dawn came many villagers walked to their fields, to inspect the damage to their crops. When they arrived, some children cutting firewood from trees fallen on the hillside called to them. The people climbed to where the children were and saw that the rain serpent had washed the earth away from a large rock, exposing a very large carving. This is the carving we today call *El Rey*.

That large bas-relief, executed on a flat vertical face of stone, is located exactly beside the large gully which carries the rainwater runoff from much of the west side of the mountain. Situated high above the site, it has a commanding view of the ancient village area, much of the central and northern valley, and the majestic Popocatepetl volcano far to the north.

plate 7

25

fig. 5, plate IV

The carving, Chalcatzingo's Monument 1, has gained the name *El Rey* (the king) because the focus of the scene is an elaborately dressed figure, seated within a large U-motif lying on its side. This motif symbolizes a cave. The addition of an oval eye on the upper edge of the cave, as well as stylized 'fangs' at its mouth, show the cave to be likewise a rendering in profile of the mouth of a supernatural earth-monster. Until the Spanish conquest, earth-monster faces served as graphic metaphors of caves, these being conceived of as entrances to the interior of the earth, the underworld, a special and sacred place which was the realm of supernatural powers, including those of fertility and rain. A more detailed discussion of this bas-relief's symbolism can be found in chapter 8.

plate 12
plates II, 12
plate 19

As the news of *El Rey* spread throughout the area, it came to the attention of archaeologist Eulalia Guzmán in Mexico City. Intrigued by the report, she soon visited Chalcatzingo. There she was shown not only *El Rey*, but also two smaller relief carvings only a few meters to the east (Monuments 6 and 8), a carved scene on a boulder at the foot of the mountain (Monument 2), and a headless statue lying in a stream bed on the terraces below (Monument 16). She recognized that two mounds on the terraced hillside were ancient pyramid structures, but she was unsure, in her report published in 1934, to which ancient culture group to attribute these finds. Little was then known of the Olmec centers and monumental art on Mexico's Gulf coast. Eulalia Guzmán's publication effectively brought Chalcatzingo to the attention of archaeologists, art historians, and the public.[9]

Although Chalcatzingo now began to gain recognition as an important site, nearly two decades passed before any archaeological research was conducted there. In 1953 the archaeologist Román Piña Chan excavated a dozen stratigraphic test pits on the terraced hillside. From the ceramics and figurines recovered he dated the earliest occupation to about 1000 BC and its close to about 200 BC, based on the chronological sequence of central Mexico as it was then understood. He felt that the site's carvings had been executed between 600 and 400 BC.[10]

My own interest in Chalcatzingo began in the mid-1960s in the course of research into the archaeology of the earliest-known farming settlements in Morelos. The investigations included analyses of the patterning of those early sites on the landscape.[11] People have always established their settlements in particular locations for specific reasons: accessibility to water, good farmland, a particular natural resource, or perhaps a defensible location was the major criterion.

The early village sites in Morelos had been located for their proximity to abundant surface water, and to humid, fertile riverbottom lands. Chalcatzingo was one of the early settlements analyzed in that study, and it proved to be an exception to the general pattern. Its eastern-Morelos location is semi-arid, lacking in fertile alluvial river deposits, and with only minimal easily accessible surface water. Since the entire Amatzinac River valley was of marginal agricultural value, the first farmers faced a greater risk of poor harvests than

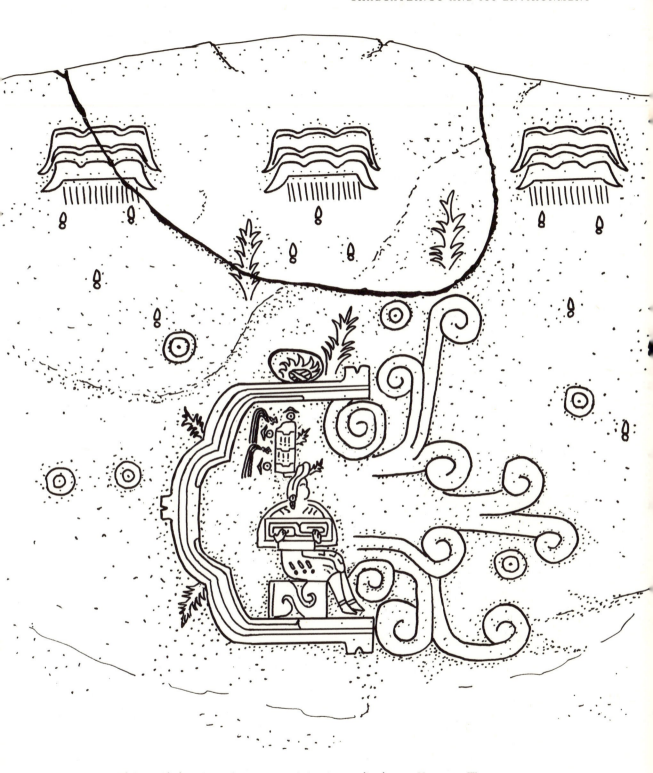

5 Monument 1, El Rey, Chalcatzingo. A personage sitting in a stylized cave. Ht 3.2 m, W. 2.7 m.

the inhabitants of well-watered valleys to the west. Yet Chalcatzingo, of all the villages in the highlands, grew rapidly to become the first major center in the region. Although agriculture could be practiced and the population sustained by local harvests, rich surpluses would not be produced. The site's importance had obviously been related to factors other than agricultural potential. To determine just what those factors were would require extensive excavations. Slowly, such a research project began to take form.

As I began sowing the ideas which would eventually grow into the excavations at Chalcatzingo, a quiet revolution was taking place in the archaeology of this early period in central Mexico.

The chronology of the Preclassic or Formative period (1500 BC–AD 200) in central Mexico was based on the pioneering archaeological investigations of George Vaillant in the 1930s.[12] The artifacts and figurines he recovered in excavations at El Arbolillo, Zacatenco, and Ticoman in the Basin of Mexico, and at Gualupita in Morelos, provided data on the basic assemblages of this period. The chronological interpretations of Vaillant, worked out when radiocarbon dating was unknown, when excavations were carried out in half-meter levels, and when screening of excavated earth was rare, had been adopted by subsequent investigators with little or no modification.

The 'Middle Preclassic period' (1000–500 BC) was commonly seen as having been characterized by small rural agricultural villages like El Arbolillo and Zacatenco. The site of Tlatilco, discovered in the early 1940s in the western suburbs of Mexico City, was seen as a more elaborate center in the midst of the rural peasantry. It consisted of a group of brickyards where workers began unearthing hundreds of human burials, many with mortuary offerings consisting of decorated and exotically shaped pottery vessels and intriguing 'pretty lady' figurines. Collectors were soon visiting the brickyards to buy artifacts, some of which looked 'Olmec.' Professional archaeologists worked on the Tlatilco cemeteries as well, and their fame spread. The site became thought of not only as a unique center for its period, but also, because of some Olmec-like artifacts, as an 'Olmec colony' in a region of relatively uncomplex farming villages.[13]

The quiet revolution challenged the existing chronology and negated the common interpretation of the data. The revolution began with the investigations of Dr Paul Tolstoy, who carried out new excavations at El Arbolillo and Tlatilco, as well as at a site in the eastern Basin, Tlapacoya. The results of that work showed that a major section of the chronological sequence was incorrect. Tlatilco, with its elaborate burial ceramics, was not contemporaneous with the 'peasant' communities of El Arbolillo and Zacatenco, but actually preceded them![14] Nor was Tlatilco unique as a site. My explorations throughout Morelos revealed that the earliest sites I was finding had burials with exotic vessels and figurines identical to those of Tlatilco. This early culture was clearly widespread in the highlands and not the result of an elite group colonizing one specific site. The exotic grave goods occurred at humble hamlets of only a few huts as well as at larger villages.[15]

Dating those early Tlatilco-like villages in Morelos confirmed the validity of Tolstoy's radically different chronological sequence. The earliest known sites, such as Tlatilco and those I was excavating in Morelos, dated to between *c.* 1200 and 900 BC, or within what we termed the Early Formative period (1500–900 BC), while sites such as Zacatenco and El Arbolillo fell within the Middle Formative period (900–500 BC). The term Preclassic was discarded because of its association with the long-established but incorrect chronology.

The quiet revolution challenged more than the central Mexican chronological sequence. Earlier, archaeologists working at early central Mexican sites had found artifacts which carried designs or stylistic motifs similar to those attributed to the ancient Olmecs of Mexico's Gulf coast. Talk of Olmec migrations and Olmec colonies in highland Mexico had appeared in the literature to explain those 'out of place' artifacts. A period of Olmec-centrism swept through scholarship. But because the quiet revolution showed the accepted dogma to be incorrect, the alleged Olmec artifacts found in the highlands came under new and more rigorous scrutiny. It was quickly discovered that they were few in number and that their importance had been greatly exaggerated. They were found primarily together with Early Formative artifacts at sites such as Tlatilco and in Morelos, but again at both tiny hamlets and large villages. Migration and colonization could barely explain this situation, for the alleged Olmec artifacts were unquestionably part of the highland cultural assemblage, manufactured locally and utilized locally. Few trade pieces could be identified. The theory that there were Gulf coast Olmec peoples in the highlands during the Early Formative period had to be abandoned.[16]

It was against this background that our project was initiated. A great quantity of questions begged for answers, both concerning Chalcatzingo as a central Mexican Formative period site and in terms of its relations with the Gulf coast. The research plan was to focus our attention on the settlement and to understand it first, for without this knowledge it would have been meaningless to seek data on external contacts and influences. It is therefore natural that house structures and archaeological remains relevant to daily life should have priority over monuments and works of art.

3 Beginning the research

Our research started at the site in January 1972. To take advantage of Mexico's dry season, each of the three major field seasons began in mid-January and ended by mid-June. During that period the agricultural fields were not covered by crops nor the excavations plagued by rain-filled pits. In addition, since the dry season is a period of relative farming inactivity by the villagers, the project supplied them with needed employment.

Arriving laden with various levels of government permits, we met the villagers and discussed the project with them, for the site lies on their communal farm lands. Their major request was that equal work opportunities should be given to all eligible village men. Because almost every rural village has a traditional communal labor system in which some participation in public works projects is required of each adult male, that communal work list became the basic employment list. A weekly rotation system, moving through all eligible village males, was agreed upon. Certain workers who exhibited special archaeological skills were retained as 'crew chiefs' each week. Soon a rotation list for female workers was also established, although village customs and strong social pressures dictated the types of jobs available to males and females.

When we started, no adequate maps of Chalcatzingo were available and, except for some of the recently farmed fields, most of the site was hidden beneath a heavy growth of tall weeds and grasses. Our first task was to clear away that overgrowth. The workers began cutting and burning the unwanted vegetation and the surface configurations of the site slowly emerged. Once that task was under way, the archaeologists working on the project spent their days walking each field and newly exposed area, noting and recording the various types of artifacts lying on the surface, but leaving the actual items untouched to await the more intensive research efforts which were to follow.

Within a very short time Chalcatzingo's amphitheater area looked entirely different. The terrace systems stood bare for the first time in perhaps a millennium. Small terraces and a variety of stone lines lay exposed where previously none had even been suspected. When we combined that fresh visual perspective with our newly acquired field-by-field data on artifact distribution, the picture of the extent of the site and its layout unfolded.

Until then the nature of Chalcatzingo was unclear. One hypothesis had been that the site was merely a religious sanctuary focused on the hillside bas-relief carvings, and that it lacked any significant occupation. The apparent absence of large mound architecture contemporaneous with the carvings suggested to some scholars that Chalcatzingo predated the architecturally rich Olmec centers on the Gulf coast, a theory which included the notion that Olmec culture originated in the highlands and later moved fully developed to the Gulf coast. Those theories died with the vegetation being cleaned from the site.[17]

Even prior to our excavations, it became clear that the terraced hillside had been the location of a village-sized settlement for many centuries. The quantity of broken pottery and maize-grinding stones indicated a substantial population, not simply a few religious specialists to care for the bas-reliefs and conduct rituals. In fact, as we studied the distribution of Middle Formative period white pottery – one of the most common types of sherds found on the surface of the terraces – an interesting pattern emerged. On each major field there was a concentration of fragments covering an area about 10 m in diameter. The regularity of the concentrations suggested to us that each might represent house refuse, and mark the location of a structure. If test excavations in these refuse areas confirmed that they were indeed house locations, we could make a major change in our research plans: rather than having to seek ancient homes through a number of laborious test excavations, we would know beforehand where they were, and could devote more time to thorough examination of the residences themselves.

It was not only possible residential areas that were exposed when the hillside was cleared of brush. What had been thought to be a small terrace rising somewhat above its neighbors was quickly seen to be a huge earthen platform mound, nearly 70 m long. Early and Middle Formative period pottery sherds eroding from the mound suggested that it was in all probability at least as old as the hillside bas-relief rock art. Although the mounds which Guzmán had seen on the site were shown by Piña Chan's excavations to date to c. AD 700,[18] Chalcatzingo was not lacking in early monumental architecture as many had presumed.

Thus the Chalcatzingo excavations began with the knowledge that house locations might already have been identified and that early monumental architecture existed at the site. But neither of these were the focus of the initial excavations. While the investigation of residential structures was a major goal of our research – for to understand Chalcatzingo meant understanding the settlement and the daily way of life of its peoples – some other fundamental problems had to be resolved archaeologically.

Of primary importance at the beginning was the development of the ceramic chronology of the site. For archaeologists working in Mexico, the sherds of broken pottery provide the most abundant and sensitive temporal markers. Vessel forms, colors, and decorations changed through time at any settlement, and a record of those changes, recovered through excavations, can provide the

Color plates *(pages 33–36)*

I Excavations on Terrace 1 during the project's first field season. In the far background is the snow-covered peak of Popocatepetl volcano.

II Monument 2, with a figure wearing an elaborate headdress, a 'bird-serpent mask,' a short cape, and holding a paddle-shaped object. Ht of figure *c.* 1 m.

III Monument 12, the 'Flying Olmec' bas-relief. Two long-tailed birds fly above the human figure, who wears an animal-face headdress. A parrot flies below the person's legs. It measures 1.4 by 1.4 m.

IV Monument 1, *El Rey*, a personage sitting in a stylized cave. Total carved area: Ht 3.2 m, W. 2.7 m.

V Monument 3, a feline (left) licking a large branching object. It measures, left to right, 1.2 m.

VI Monument 4, two highly stylized felines pounce on two prone human figures. The carving has fallen partly on its side. It measures 2.5 by 2.5 m.

VII Excavating the tabletop altar and patio area on Terrace 25. A burial lies exposed in front of the altar.

VIII La Venta Altar 4, an Olmec tabletop altar showing a royal personage seated in the frontal niche, holding ropes passing to persons carved in bas-relief on the sides. Ht 1.6 m.

I

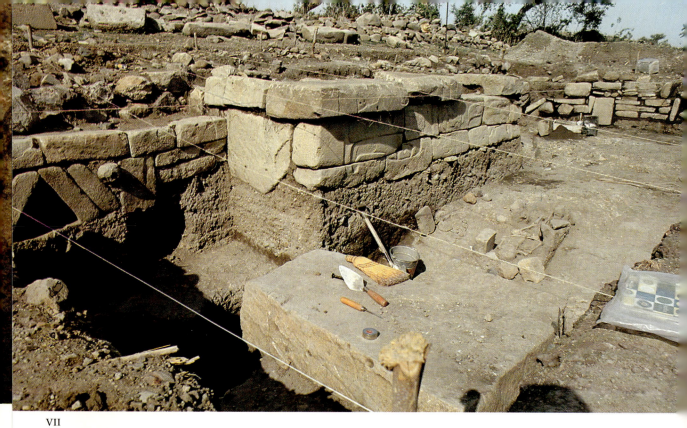

VII

VIII

archaeologist with basic chronological control. Even in the absence of absolute dates provided by radiocarbon samples, the types of pottery recovered can offer a good idea of where a deposit fits within the relative sequence, and which deposits are contemporaneous with others. Without the checks provided by a good ceramic chronology the archaeologist might make erroneous comparisons (as in the case of considering Tlatilco contemporaneous with El Arbolillo and Zacatenco), and draw the wrong conclusions.

Piña Chan's excavations two decades earlier had concentrated primarily on one of the site's largest and uppermost terraces, a field we labeled Terrace 1.[19] The large platform mound revealed by the brush-clearing operation forms the northern (downhill) border of that terrace. His test pits indicated deeper deposits there than on other terraces, and for our ceramic sequence we desired the longest (deepest) stratigraphic record possible. Thus our first excavations at Chalcatzingo focused on Terrace 1. A transect line, or trench, was laid out beginning on the platform mound at the terrace's north side and running due south to the talus slopes of the Cerro Chalcatzingo which delimit Terrace 1's south side. Trenches 3 m long and 1 m wide were begun at 10-m intervals along this transect line. Each of the trenches was carefully excavated to the rock-hard sterile soil (*tepetate*), which usually lay about 4 m below the surface. The stratigraphy visible in the side of the trench was then carefully studied and mapped, and soil samples were taken from each major level. The samples were later processed to extract any fossil pollen remains, since these would provide a history of changing vegetation patterns, which in turn might tell us about climatic shifts and human disturbance of the landscape.

When an individual trench was completed, it was then extended by excavating the next 3-m section along the transect line. As time progressed the various trenches and their extensions grew into a nearly complete cross trench bisecting Terrace 1. The stratified deposits provided the data needed to construct a basic ceramic chronology, although that chronology continued to be revised and refined throughout the project.

The cross trench uncovered several buried walls and one stone structure. It also cut into the face of the large platform mound. The ceramics recovered from the mound's interior demonstrated without question that its outer levels were Middle Formative. The structure was not only unique for its time in central Mexico, but the possibility remained that even earlier structures underlay the mound's Middle Formative levels.

Following the digging of trenches on Terrace 1, which occupied a good portion of the first field season, the excavations were expanded and intensified. To our great pleasure, trial excavations in the ceramic concentrations showed that our hypothesis was correct, and stone house foundations lay beneath the surface. Yet we were also forced to accept an unfortunate fact. Twenty-five hundred years of erosion and redeposition had taken place in essentially equal proportions. This meant that the floors of houses built in 700 or 600 BC were

plate 1

still at about the level of the present-day ground surface, and had been destroyed not only by natural forces such as erosion, but also by several centuries of ploughing. Archaeologists are able to understand a great deal about a house through the patterned way in which artifacts are distributed on a living floor. At Chalcatzingo the pattern had been lost. All that remained of most residential structures were their stone foundations. Luckily, some data, such as burials placed beneath house floors, had survived and were still recoverable.

So much time was taken up with the task of excavating that we soon gave up the idea of making the topographic map of the site ourselves. A Mexican firm was contracted, which used the technique of photogrammetry as the basis for mapping.[20] This method employs stereographic aerial photographs, from which the map is drawn in the laboratory with complex instruments. The maps produced had contour intervals of 1 m, and were as accurate as any which could have been made using a transit survey. The photogrammetric maps easily provided contours of the rugged mountains which tower over the site. To map the *cerros* by any other means would have been a nearly impossible task.

Aerial photographs also assisted us in a separate phase of the Chalcatzingo work – our regional reconnaissance. Most archaeological research is limited, through constraints of time and money, to investigations at one particular site. Yet no ancient settlement existed in a cultural vacuum, without daily contact with other nearby communities. Chalcatzingo's local interaction area was the valley of the Amatzinac River and, to understand the development of Chalcatzingo's social and political position within the valley, we complemented our investigations with a reconnaissance of the entire valley, an area of approximately 210 sq. miles.

We purchased aerial photographs with a scale of 1:5000 from an agency of the Mexican government, and a group of project members spent nearly six months walking almost every field in the valley, plotting on those large photos the location of all visible archaeological features they found, whether simply a scatter of ceramics or a complex grouping of large mounds. Specially prepared recording sheets were filled in to provide information on the size and period of the site (identified through the ceramic sherds found), as well as data on mounds, ecology, and topography. Over 300 sites were recorded, covering a time range of about 3000 years, from *c.* 1500 BC to after the Spanish conquest in AD 1521.

The data gathered by this extensive reconnaissance allowed us to document the history of settlement in the valley. By classifying each site according to size and periods of habitation, and by placing those data on maps, we gained a visual record of population growth and cultural development in the valley. Some sites grew larger over time while others flourished momentarily and then declined. For each period we have an idea of Chalcatzingo's comparative importance in the valley.[21]

From those diverse sources of data we can today reconstruct a greal deal about the site, its evolution from a tiny settlement to a center of inter-regional importance, and we have discovered more about the life of its people. At its apogee, late in the Middle Formative period, Chalcatzingo was clearly the major center in the highlands, and maintained close economic and cultural ties with one or more of the major, Gulf coast Olmec centers. At the same time, the archaeological record shows that culturally it was a central Mexican site, yet manifesting a small but highly visible set of Gulf coast traits primarily related to ritual and elite activities. The evidence suggests that during its period of power one or more of its rulers had entered into significant alliances with the Olmec, possibly through marriage, and that perhaps some leaders were themselves Gulf coast elite who had assumed control for the purpose of directing the acquisition and shipment of various highland raw materials desired by their distant homeland.

Chalcatzingo was culturally central Mexican as I have said, and to the few Gulf coast people who may have arrived there it would have seemed far different from the Olmec heartland, a veritable frontier zone. For this reason I occasionally use the term 'frontier' to lend a special meaning to certain Gulf coast-like aspects of the site, and particularly the carved monuments which can be better understood in that light.

4 From hamlet to regional center

The earliest evidence for human occupation of the hillside came from the deepest levels in two stratigraphic pits excavated into the top of the site's large earthen platform mound. Each excavation reached sterile soil at about 5 m; a small quantity of ceramics came from the level just above the sterile *tepetate*. Most of these sherds are from simple polished brown bowls whose only decoration consisted of a band of red paint around their rim. Flecks of charcoal collected from this same level produced a radiocarbon date of 1660 BC ± 90 years. This is one of the earliest dates known for ceramics in central Mexico, but must be viewed with caution because although this small group of sherds shows great similarities in form, color, and decoration to very early ceramics from Zohapilco in the Basin of Mexico and from the site of San José Mogote in the valley of Oaxaca,[22] a date from a single radiocarbon assay cannot be considered definitive; multiple dates are preferred. But we are left with the knowledge that the settlement at Chalcatzingo is of great antiquity.

The first period for which there is well-documented evidence of substantial occupation was named by our ceramicist the Amate phase, *c.* 1500–1100 BC. Unfortunately we found few primary, undisturbed Amate phase deposits. Most had been destroyed by later episodes of terrace construction. Amate phase levels, because they are the earliest, are also deeply buried under later deposits. Due to these factors our excavations did not locate any houses or burials from that period. However, the surface distribution of Amate phase artifacts, together with the disturbed Amate phase levels found in excavations, have allowed us to determine that the community at that time covered a limited area of unmodified hillside. It was probably a hamlet with a population of no more than sixty individuals.

Amate phase ceramics are like those found at Tlatilco in the Basin of Mexico and at Early Formative period sites elsewhere in Morelos.[23] The assemblage includes a variety of brown bowls and bottles decorated with linear red designs. Only a few sherds of typical Tlatilco exotic bottle forms were found, but it must be remembered that those from Tlatilco had been mortuary offerings, and we found no Amate phase burials. Amate phase figurines include 'pretty ladies' and a very few of the babyface figurines also frequently identified as 'Olmec' but common in central Mexico at this time.

plates 47–9

In its ceramics there is nothing to distinguish Chalcatzingo's assemblage from those of other sites in the region. The site differs, however, in one respect: monumental architecture. There are two examples, neither of which were completely excavated. The first was uncovered while excavating the deep pits into the upper surface of the long platform mound. Those excavations penetrated earlier structures which had been covered by the platform. The oldest of those constructions, an earthen mound with a facing of stone cobbles, had been built atop the levels containing the early pottery mentioned above. Built sometime during the Amate phase, it was originally more than 2 m high, and had been further enlarged at least once during that time, nearly doubling its height. Other enlargements took place in subsequent phases, culminating about 600 BC in the large platform visible today.

A second and smaller structure was found on Terrace 6, a terrace below and to the east of Terrace 1. That construction is a small platform mound, possibly rectangular in shape and standing slightly over 1 m high. It was also faced with stone cobbles and irregular rocks. Found in a brief investigation carried out in 1976 to clarify the Amate phase ceramic chronology, it would have been impossible to excavate the structure adequately in the time available and was thus reburied to await future research at the site.

The presence of such mound architecture at Chalcatzingo at a period when it was all but unknown elsewhere in the central highlands, poses an enigma. In comparison to western and central Morelos and the southern Basin of Mexico, the valley of the Amatzinac River was clearly less attractive for settlement because of its marginal agricultural potential. Our data bear this out, for only eight small Amate phase sites were found during our reconnaissance of the valley, a tiny number compared with those in agriculturally richer areas of the region. In fact, it is probable that the Amatzinac valley was not significantly inhabited until population growth to the north and west created land pressures and justified expansion into agriculturally less promising areas. Why then did one of the valley's eight hamlets, Chalcatzingo, have this special architecture, when it has yet to be found at larger sites in richer areas?

The question will remain unanswered until further data can be gathered on this period both at Chalcatzingo and at contemporaneous settlements throughout Morelos. Such architecture may exist at those other and often larger sites, but has yet to be found and correctly dated. On the other hand, Chalcatzingo may already have assumed a significant role in the inter-regional distribution of important raw materials. I suspect both will be found to be true.

The following period was named by our ceramicist the Barranca phase, which began in about 1100 BC and continued until about 700 BC. It was at about 1100 BC that a change in ceramic styles began in central Mexico. Brown vessels, including exotic bottles decorated with linear red designs, gradually gave way to white ceramics. These new wares were commonly decorated along their rims with an incised design which has become known as the

6 *Amatzinac White bowl with rim decorated in a variant of the double-line-break motif. The interior base of the bowl is also decorated. Diam. 25.5 cm.*

fig. 6   'double-line-break' motif. A great deal of variation occurs within the motifs lumped under that name, but basically the motif consists of a set of parallel lines circling the rim, with one line 'broken' in places by gaps.[24]

A second ceramic type, which can be called 'differentially fired' ware, began increasing in popularity at that same time. Its potters demonstrated their great skills by carefully manipulating the firing atmospheres in their simple kilns.

7 *Pavon Fine Grey bowl. Rim diam. 22 cm.*

Most differentially fired vessels are black (requiring an oxygen-starved kiln atmosphere) while the rim is white (needing an oxygen-rich one). The colors could also be reversed, but in either instance, the dichotomy probably had symbolic value. Differentially fired ceramics are not confined to central Mexico, since they were common in much of the area to the south as well.

At Chalcatzingo several new local pottery styles developed, a few of which were adopted elsewhere in the highlands, perhaps through Chalcatzingo's influence. These included a distinctive orange pottery, Peralta Orange, and a second orange ware with a lacquer-like appearance.

One problem faced by archaeologists is the determination of whether a new pottery type appearing in the stratigraphic record represents a local innovation or a type typical of another area and perhaps imported through trade. Many archaeologists have depended on educated guesses in these instances, but if their judgment were incorrect, the hypotheses generated from those guesses would be equally suspect. In fact the tenuous nature of such hypotheses is frequently left unclear in some scholarly publications, and an educated guess occasionally becomes an accepted 'truth.'

At Chalcatzingo this problem was partially solved through microscopic analyses of the clay and mineral inclusions in the sherds of each pottery type.[25] Inclusions such as sand were added to clay during the pottery manufacturing process to reduce shrinkage, and the minerals used will obviously differ with a region's geology. The clay and sands of the Amatzinac valley derive from igneous rocks, and there is very little variation throughout the various pottery types found at the site.

However, a significant stranger in the midst of Chalcatzingo's Barranca phase pottery was a well-made grey ware, Pavon Fine Grey. Its inclusions *fig. 7* come from an area of metamorphic rocks, indicating that in all probability the pottery had been manufactured at least 40 miles east or southeast of the Amatzinac valley, in the states of Puebla or northern Oaxaca. Not surprisingly, grey pottery was far more common in that region, a further reason to suggest it as the source area.

While grey ware was common to the east, not every grey pot or sherd recovered at Chalcatzingo was an 'import.' Near the middle of the Barranca phase a grey ware manufactured from local clay (and inclusions) appeared in the ceramic sequence. While perhaps copying the imported grey pottery, it did not replace it. Both continued to be used through the remainder of the Barranca phase and through the subsequent Cantera phase as well.

Early in the Barranca phase a most significant event took place at Chalcatzingo: the terracing of the hillsides. Their construction involved a great amount of planning and human labor, and was carried out through a number of 'cut-and-fill' operations, using nothing more complicated than sharpened wooden poles, and baskets or animal skins for carrying the soil. At the place designated for a terrace, upslope soil was loosened with sharpened poles and carried a slight distance downslope, where it was dumped. The terrace was created simply by removing soil from the upper part of an area, thus making it lower, and at the same time raising the downslope area by adding fill dirt there. As one area was lowered and the other raised they eventually reached the same level and formed a flat terrace. Our Terrace 1 excavations show that there the upslope was cut completely down to bedrock. Such cutting and dumping of great quantities of earth destroyed many of the Amate phase deposits on the old natural hillside, and buried others under deep deposits of fill. But these very actions are such that we can date fairly precisely when the terracing was accomplished.

The construction work involved a great expenditure of human labor. It is possible that additional earth for the terraces was brought up from the base of the hill, basket-load by basket-load. However, while a great many working hours were certainly involved, the number of people required may not have been so large. Our dating techniques are presently not precise enough to permit us to date decade by decade when each terrace unit was constructed, but we may be witnessing construction activities which took several decades to complete. On a year-by-year basis the terraces could have been built by the villagers themselves, with little or no need for outside assistance from neighboring settlements.

Terraces of the type found at Chalcatzingo usually occur in regions of low annual rainfall, since they were built to maximize the amount of rainwater retained on the fields. Without modern techniques such as contour ploughing, hillside farm plots lost much of the precious rainfall through runoff.[26] The hillsides at Chalcatzingo were vulnerable to such losses and the flat fields created by terracing would have solved that problem. Analysis of fossil pollen collected by us from Barranca phase strata on Terrace 1 indicates that the climate then was drier than at present. The need for rainwater retention would have been more acute.

At the same time, erosion from heavy rains would have endangered the newly terraced fields, and protective safeguards were included in the terrace constructions, demonstrating foresight and careful planning on the part of the builders. Then, as today, almost all the rain falling on the Cerro Chalcatzingo and Cerro Delgado collects in a few natural mountainside channels and flows directly downhill towards the terraced amphitheater area. During a rainstorm, the volume of water flowing in those channels is surprising. If not controlled it would have flooded and washed away major areas of some terraces.

Monument 1, the so-called *El Rey* relief on the side of the Cerro Chalcatzingo, sits adjacent to that mountain's major natural runoff channel. Far below *El Rey*, just before the channel reaches the terraces, it is modified by a large artificial embankment which turns it through ninety degrees, toward the east and away from the fields. A similar but even more massive water-control construction occurs further downhill, on a channel beginning on the east side of Terrace 1 which carries runoff from both mountains. During heavy rains we have seen this watercourse fill to a depth of 2 m with rushing water. The diversion on this channel is 7 m tall and 35 m long. It was built as an integral part of the terrace system. The sharp right-angles constructed in both diversion embankments are still capable of blunting the force of any torrent of runoff water, slowing and controlling its rush down the hill to the flatlands and towards the small stream running to the *barranca* of the Amatzinac River. Modern farmers continue to keep the channel clear of debris and in operating condition, for they are aware of the system's efficacy.

plate 8

From the distribution of Barranca phase ceramics and utilitarian artifacts it appears that the terraces were used both for farming and habitation, a pattern which will be discussed more completely in chapter 6. The community at that time was probably a small village with a population of between 130 and 325 people, a slow but sizeable population increase from the Amate phase.

Terrace 1 remained the focal point of the community, for there the public architecture was located. The platform mound on the north edge of Terrace 1 was probably enlarged during that period, while a second, smaller platform was built to the south of it. Although only exposed in test excavations, the second structure appears to parallel the big mound, in a configuration reminiscent of later Mesoamerican ballcourts. More excavations will be needed before the ballcourt possibility can be seriously examined.

The only complete house of the Barranca phase found and excavated was situated within the modern ploughzone level, and the large irregular stones used in its foundation protruded above the surface of the field. If the stone lines which crossed the structure identify interior walls, the quadrangular house, which covered an area of 27.5 sq. m, had three rooms. One room, containing the remnants of a hearth and a small deposit of buried refuse, can be identified as the cooking area.

Scattered among the soil excavated from the house interior were small chunks of clay, smoothed on one side but with impressions of thick finger-sized plant stalks on the opposite side. These tell us that the house had cane walls which had been coated with mud plaster. Such 'wattle and daub' walls were typical of later houses at the site as well.

During the Barranca phase the population increased not only at Chalcatzingo but throughout the valley. During the Amate phase most of the settlements had been in the northern valley, the area with greater annual rainfall. Only one small community was located by our reconnaissance in the south. In the Barranca phase the number of northern settlements doubled, but five new communities appeared in the southern valley. Almost all the new settlements were small hamlets, but Chalcatzingo and two others had grown to village size. A similar population growth occurred simultaneously in the Basin of Mexico.

Very little archaeological data are available from the Basin on communities at the period equivalent to the Barranca phase. Excavations by Niederberger at Zohapilco, a settlement which had been located adjacent to the lake in the southeast portion of the Basin, provide the best stratigraphic record yet available, but no data on houses, social organization, etc. Zohapilco, like the community at Zacatenco, the site first excavated by Vaillant and more recently by Tolstoy, seems typical of the farming culture common throughout the highlands at that time.[27]

The elaborate burial cult which had characterized Tlatilco and other highland Early Formative sites was no longer an important part of the people's ritual practices. Burials throughout the region received fewer and less ornate ceramic vessels. While the mortuary goods lacked the flamboyance of the Tlatilco offerings, that should not be interpreted as an impoverishment of the culture. It probably reflects simply a de-emphasis of the deceased's social ranking, role, and kin or clan affiliations displayed through mortuary pottery.

Chalcatzingo reached its apogee between 700 and 500 BC, both in its size and in the elaborateness of its culture. By this period, which was named by our ceramicist the Cantera phase, Chalcatzingo had become a major regional center and possibly the most important site in central Mexico. While it may have attained such regional importance earlier, it is now that its status becomes clearly apparent in the archaeological record. A number of special-purpose stone-faced structures were built as the public-ritual area more than doubled in extent. The occupation zone stretched beyond the terraces onto the valley floor and to lands on the other side of the Cerro Delgado.

Most if not all of Chalcatzingo's famed carvings were probably executed during the Cantera phase, but their dating is difficult. Reliefs carved high on the mountainside and on large boulders on the talus slopes are impossible to date by known archaeological means. Constant erosion has long ago stripped away any sherds or offerings which might have been associated with them and which may have assisted in their dating. However, certain artistic conventions employed in the reliefs show strong similarities with Gulf coast Olmec carvings from the same time as the Cantera phase. Dating various monuments discovered by our excavations on the terraces themselves is more certain. They occur in good Cantera phase contexts. Both the hillside reliefs and the newly uncovered monuments are discussed in later chapters.

The major ceramics of the Barranca phase continued into the Cantera phase, with changes occurring principally in vessel forms. The continuity in ceramics during the 600 years of these two phases allows us to presume a similar continuity and indigenous evolution of culture at the site. Change is marked mainly by growth and elaboration, both at Chalcatzingo and throughout the Amatzinac valley.

Forty-nine settlements existed in the valley during the Cantera phase. Besides Chalcatzingo, the sites that were largest and most important were still located in the northern valley; and although Chalcatzingo, with its carvings and monumental architecture, remained unique in central Mexico, its influence was strongly felt by its local neighbors. Several other sites in the valley possessed mound architecture, but presumably these were secondary centers, below Chalcatzingo in the hierarchy of communities. Their rulers were probably tied to those of Chalcatzingo through kinship and trade, and were consciously emulating the larger center. This same hierarchical pattern has not been found in other areas of Morelos or the Basin of Mexico.[28] Cantera phase Chalcatzingo had no clear rival elsewhere in the highlands.

Chalcatzingo's role as the major highland center rapidly diminished after 500 BC, and the settlement was soon abandoned. As will be discussed later, its decline may be linked at least in part to sociopolitical changes taking place throughout Mesoamerica at this time, including the rise of new power centers throughout central and southern Mexico.

The majority of the Chalcatzingo excavations dealt with Cantera phase residential and public structures, mainly because the Cantera phase deposits are overwhelmingly abundant. This period, from 700 to 500 BC, saw Chalcatzingo's maximum importance. The next chapter discusses the site's Cantera phase monumental and public architecture and the monuments associated with public-ritual areas. Chapter 6 then deals with residential architecture and the burials found within the dwellings and elsewhere.

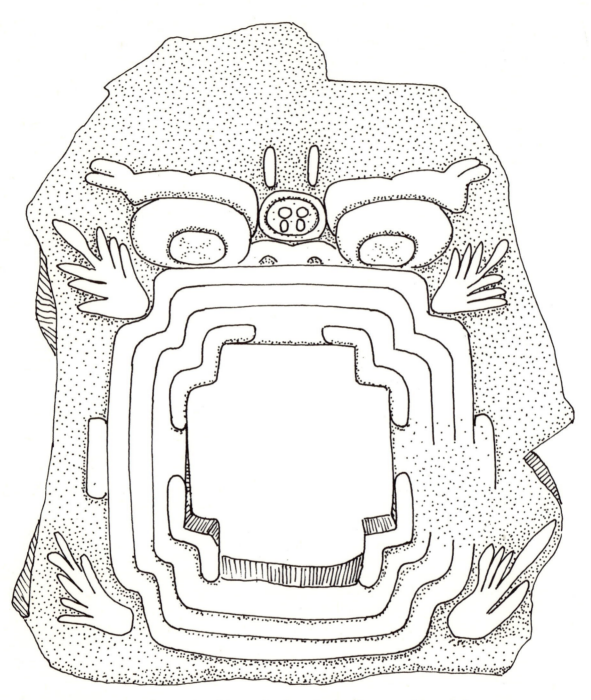

8 *Monument 9, a free-standing slab carved with a stylized earth-monster face symbolizing a cave. Ht 1.8 m, W. 1.5 m.*

5 Public architecture and political monuments

Terrace 1, a large upper terrace directly below the hillside bas-relief carvings of the Cerro Chalcatzingo, was the focus of the village's elite and ritual activities. Just as the area serving residential structures gradually increased, so too did that devoted to public and elite functions. Dwellings on the terraces just below Terrace 1 gave way to special stone-faced platform mounds as the Cantera phase public area expanded.

Of all the monumental or public structures at the site, the large earthen platform mound on the northern edge of Terrace 1 was certainly the most important. It is the only public structure whose several rebuildings span over 600 years. This alone attests to its principal role. Its size and form too are significant. Approximately 70 m in length, with a relatively flat upper surface about 30 m wide, the platform closely resembles platform mounds at San Lorenzo, La Venta, and Laguna de los Cerros, all major Olmec centers on the Gulf coast.

Although slightly modified by a later culture group about AD 700, the platform's earthen construction remained relatively unchanged. Its upper surface area has been ploughed and planted for at least the past 100 years, effectively destroying most remaining constructions on this huge platform. However, some idea of what originally existed can be deduced from objects recently found lying on or near the mound. For example, large rectangular blocks of faced stone occur today near the base of the platform, tumbled down to their present location by farmers who over the years removed stones from the top of this 'raised field' which were a hindrance to their planting. Our excavations also uncovered three similar large rectangular stones buried by the farmers along the sides of the platform. The original location of all these stones seems to have been the mound's upper surface, although whether they had been parts of a construction, or were set up individually as small monuments cannot presently be determined.

One and possibly other carved monuments had been erected on the platform. Like the rectangular blocks lying at the base of the mound, the headless statue found by Guzmán in approximately the same area may once have stood on top of the platform.[29] But while that is speculative, the discovery of Monument 9 on the structure itself provides more positive evidence. This

plate 19

49

carving was found in the early 1960s by a farmer preparing a field for planting. It consisted of a number of broken fragments buried at the north edge of the mound's upper surface. The farmer removed the pieces to his house in the village and eventually sold them. From Chalcatzingo they made their way (pieced together) onto the international antiquities market. Today the reconstructed monument is on display at an art institute in New York State.

fig. 8

Monument 9 is a large but relatively thin quadrangular stone slab approximately 1.8 m tall and 1.5 m wide, meant to stand in an upright position. The bas-relief carving covering its surface depicts the face of a zoomorphic earth-monster in frontal view. The face is dominated by a yawning cruciform mouth. A mouth of the same shape, in profile, characterizes the cave niche of Monument 1 (*El Rey*), described in chapter 8. The cave/interior-of-the-earth symbolism is identical therefore in Monument 9, but carried one step further. The interior of the mouth is an actual cruciform opening which passes completely through the rock slab. Interestingly, the base of this opening is slightly worn down, as if people or objects had passed through the mouth as part of rituals associated with the monument.

plate 28

The large, centrally located platform mound obviously served as a focal point of public ritual. We also discovered that it was the burial place of some of the community's highest-ranking functionaries. Two burials fortuitously discovered in our test excavations of the platform were richer in jade jewelry than any other uncovered on the site. Near to these, the excavations disclosed a low stone wall with a narrow 'doorway' sealed with stones. This construction proved to be the front of a tomb-like grave unlike any known in Mesoamerica at this time. Behind the wall was a mound of stone cobbles covering the interment. Unfortunately, our excitement was quickly dashed when we found indications of relatively recent looting. The grave had been discovered and plundered several years before our research. One piece of apple-green jade, apparently once part of a mosaic disk, lay among the human bone fragments in the churned earth of the tomb's interior. Later we heard rumors of a 'stone statue' removed by the looters.

plate 4

Extending southwards from the base of the platform mound is the large plaza-like area of Terrace 1. Evidence suggests that this large space functioned as a public and ritual area. On its south side, separated by almost 100 m from the platform mound, stood the village's major elite residence and two related structures. The traits singling out that particular dwelling and its inhabitants as different and special are discussed in chapter 6, but we hypothesize that the residence and its auxiliary buildings served the site's ruler.

fig. 9

That plan, consisting of a central plaza-like public area lying between a large public mound and a special chiefly residence, is not unique to Cantera phase Chalcatzingo. An analogous and contemporaneous pattern occurs at the site of San José Mogote, Oaxaca, and will probably be recognized at other major Middle Formative period sites as their internal structuring becomes better understood.[30]

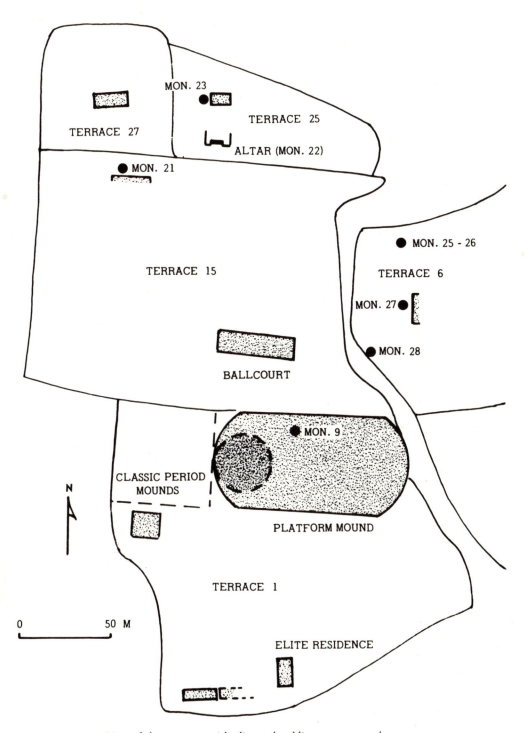

9 Map of the terraces, with elite and public structures and monuments.

Color plates *(pages 53–56)*

IX Olmec colossal stone head from the site of San Lorenzo. Ht 2.85 m.

X Three Late Formative period figurines (*c.* 300 BC) found in a burial intruding into a Middle Formative period platform on Terrace 27. Ht 13 cm.

XI Hollow white ceramic baby figure, of unspecified Gulf coast provenance. Ht *c.* 30 cm.

XII San Lorenzo Monument 52, a werejaguar figure carved on the outer surface of a U-shaped drain stone. Ht 90 cm.

XIII Jade earspools worn by an elite person buried atop the large platform mound. Diam. *c.* 2.5 cm.

XIV Werejaguar figurine from a crypt burial beneath the floor of the elite residence on Terrace 1. Ht 11 cm.

XV Olmec colossal stone head from the site of La Venta. Ht 2.4 m.

As already mentioned, Terrace 1 was always the center of public and ritual activities, and, during the Cantera phase, adjacent terraces assumed similar roles as the public quarter underwent expansion. The three terraces below Terrace 1 became the location of special architectural constructions: rectangular stone-faced platform mounds each with at least one carved stela in association.

The size and elaborateness of the platforms varies. The largest and best preserved is found on Terrace 6. This structure, running in a north-south direction, consists of a two-stepped façade of stone cobbles, 15.7 m long, with two side walls each about 3 m in length. It apparently had no actual back wall, but was a three-sided structure which protruded from the sloping hillside. The structure had been rebuilt several times by adding new façades. Although the total height today is 1.3 m, the upper walls are in the plough zone and the original height may have been somewhat greater.

plate 21

The events leading to the discovery of this particular platform confirm the role of luck in some archaeological research. The farmer who had for years planted this field (as well as Terrace 1) was never in favor of our research, although his crops were not endangered. His attitude gradually changed, however, and one morning, about half-way through our third and final season, he visited the excavations and then asked us to walk with him to Terrace 6. There, in the midst of the rock-littered field, he pointed to one of the many stones protruding from the surface and showed us its faint carved lines. These were not recent scratches made by ploughing, but the weathered remains of a carved relief. Clearing around the stone revealed that it was the mere tip of a carving which continued downward.

As soon as we could, excavations were begun, and they quickly revealed that this was not a broken fragment lying randomly in the plough zone, but a large stela, partly mutilated but still standing in place. As the area was enlarged, a small section of stone wall directly behind the stela was found to continue in both directions. This eventually turned out to be the front wall of the platform.

The stela, Monument 27, depicts a standing figure in left profile, with legs apart as if walking. Worn or draped over the shoulder is an animal skin or perhaps the entire animal, probably a deer. The animal's hind legs, with cloven hooves, hang downwards and extend towards the front edge of the monument. The person's left arm is bent to hold a long and thick bundle or scepter-like object. The figure's stance and the large 'scepter' held in the left arm are characteristic of a number of frontier 'Olmec-style' carvings, but the single 'walking' individual holding a 'scepter' is not found in heartland monumental art.

fig. 10

The individuals on the frontier monuments sometimes have their faces shown, as in the four separate carvings at the site of Chalchuapa, El Salvador, or they may wear a distinctive type of mask which usually covers their lower face, the so-called bird-serpent mask, such as is seen on the carving at Xoc, in

fig. 11

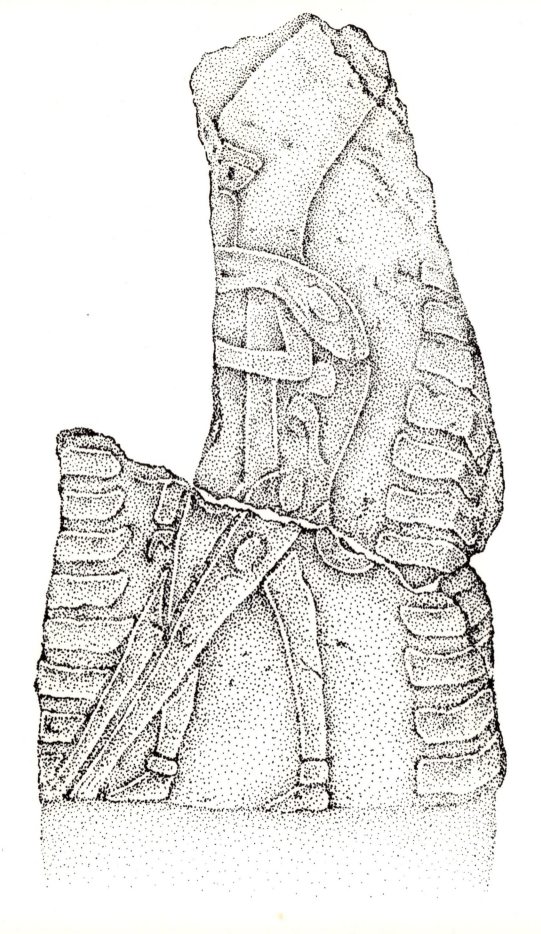

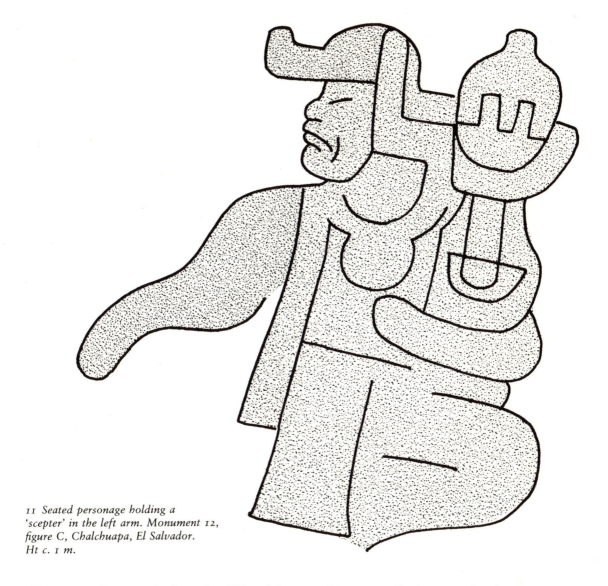

11 *Seated personage holding a 'scepter' in the left arm. Monument 12, figure C, Chalchuapa, El Salvador. Ht c. 1 m.*

Chiapas, and on a stela from San Miguel Amuco, Guerrero.[31] In the case of   plate 11
Chalcatzingo's Monument 27, the face is missing, for at some time in the site's
history the stela was desecrated by breaking it into three parts. The section
containing the face was removed from the area. Monument mutilation was a
common practice at Gulf coast centers, and the frontier Olmec-style
monuments were not immune to such destruction: sites such as Abaj Takalik
in Guatemala, Padre Piedra in Chiapas, and Chalcatzingo, have all such
mutilated carvings. An analysis of Chalcatzingo's mutilated art aids in

10 *(Opposite) Monument 27, a walking personage wearing an animal skin and holding a rod-like bundle in the left arm.*

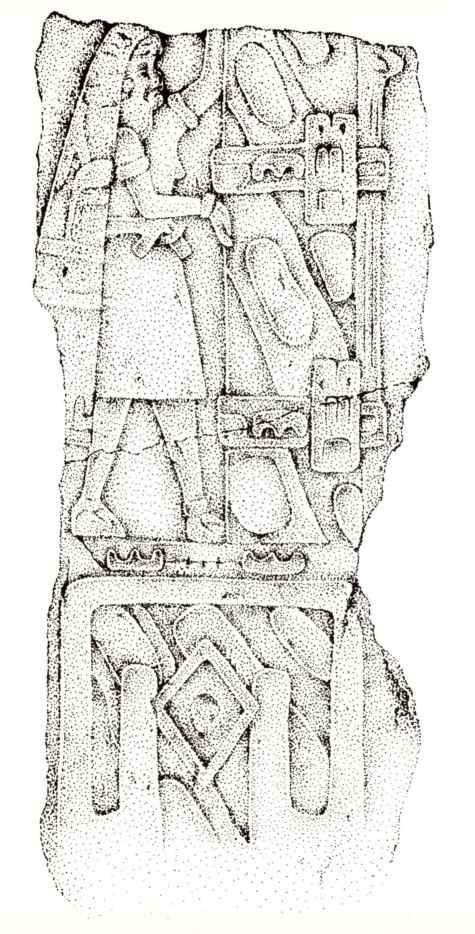

understanding the purpose of such monument destruction and is discussed in chapter 10.

Directly to the west of Terrace 6, across a drainage gully, is Terrace 15, a field directly south of and below the site's large earthen platform mound. At this terrace's north edge a large stela was discovered lying face down, barely exposed by plough furrows. This find, when excavated, disclosed another stone-faced platform, which, like the Terrace 6 structure, has a façade and two sidewalls, but no rear (uphill) wall. It is 19.5 m in length and is aligned east-west, parallel to the face of the terrace. It is only 1 m in height since, like other Chalcatzingo architecture, its upper surface has been destroyed by ploughing so that its original vertical dimension cannot be determined.

Although the stela (Monument 21) associated with the stone-faced platform of Terrace 15 had fallen from its original standing position, excavations on the platform discovered a small stone structure which had helped to support the carving, which did not have a deeply buried base. Thus its original position is known.

The carving itself depicts the right profile of a standing woman. Her legs are *fig. 12* apart in a 'walking' stance, but she is probably not advancing, because in front of her is a tall rectangular pillar-like object that she touches with her outstretched hands. She wears only a skirt and her upper torso is bare, disclosing that she is female. Because other personages depicted at Chalcatzingo (e.g. *El Rey*) and on Gulf coast monuments sometimes wear skirt-like garments, they have been called 'female,' although we have no proof that such garments were worn by women alone. The clearly depicted breast on Chalcatzingo's woman leaves no doubt as to her gender, and makes this the earliest known carving of a female in Mesoamerica.

The third stone-faced platform is four sided. It is located at the north end of Terrace 25, immediately to the north and slightly below Terrace 15. Although 16.5 m long and 4.5 m wide, it is today only 50 cm tall. Its stela (Monument 23) had been mutilated and only the uncarved base remained in place at the time of our excavations.

I argued in an article published in 1981 that stelae and many other carvings at Chalcatzingo and Gulf coast Olmec centers were often portraits of individuals, usually a center's ruler. These specific personages can be identified by a major design motif usually carried in their headdresses.[32] If that hypothesis is correct, then the presence of portrait stelae in front of the three stone-faced platform structures implies the platforms were in some way specially connected with the individuals portrayed.

A refuse pit found intruding into the interior of the Terrace 25 platform suggests that each platform may have served as the base for an elite residential

12 (Opposite) Monument 21, a woman facing a tall object, and standing above a stylized earth-monster face. Ht 2.4 m.

structure, perhaps the home of the person depicted on the stelae. Of course, alternative hypotheses are numerous. For instance, each platform might have been a ritual construction used by a particular lineage, with its leader personified in the carving. Or the platforms may be the shrines of deceased rulers, although the mutilation pattern suggests that such is not the case.

There is no reason to believe that the platforms are exactly contemporaneous, and when ceramic chronologies have been refined so that the temporal differences become apparent, the sequence of their construction may illuminate for the first time a succession of rulers and their portrait stelae.

In attempting to understand the function of the platforms and their stelae it is important to know that some evidence suggests that a ruler may have had several monuments erected during his lifetime. On the other hand, a single terrace and platform served perhaps several rulers of the same lineage. The data leading to these assumptions come from Terrace 6, location of the stone-faced platform with its mutilated stela (Monument 27) still in situ. Two other stelae, Monuments 28 and 26, were also found on that terrace and both could predate Monument 27.

Monument 28 is the largest of Chalcatzingo's known stelae. It was found on the southwest side of the terrace, where its top section had been exposed by the rainwater drainage channel that separates Terraces 6 and 15. The carving was *fig. 13* in very low relief and is eroded and indistinct. A rubbing taken of the monument enhanced the faint details sufficiently to show that it depicts a standing personage against a background of design elements which seem to represent plumes. The face of the figure had apparently been destroyed by being ground away, a common means of mutilation on Gulf coast monuments which were too large to break.

Monuments 28 and 27 are dissimilar in their form and their carved personages. Although Monument 28 cannot be dated, the fact that it is buried a few meters from where Monument 27 still stands suggests it predates the erection of Monument 27. Monument 28 may therefore have once stood in front of an earlier building stage of the platform and have depicted a ruler slightly earlier in date than the person of Monument 27. That could indicate that the individuals were of the same genealogy or lineage.

Monument 26 was found to the north of the platform, near the edge of the terrace. Only the base of the stela remained in situ, the main body having been broken off and buried elsewhere on the site. Thus we have no carved record of the personage depicted on the missing section. The positioning of this stela, due north of the platform, as well as its stratigraphic position, imply that it may relate to one of the most recent platform rebuildings. In execution and size it is most similar to Monument 26, and not the finely carved Monument 27 which still stands at the platform's face.

Monument 26 had been erected beside another carving, Monument 25, a *fig. 14* circular 'altar' 1.3 m in diameter and 50 cm tall. Carved around its upper circumference are pendant ovals, beneath which an undulating line circles the

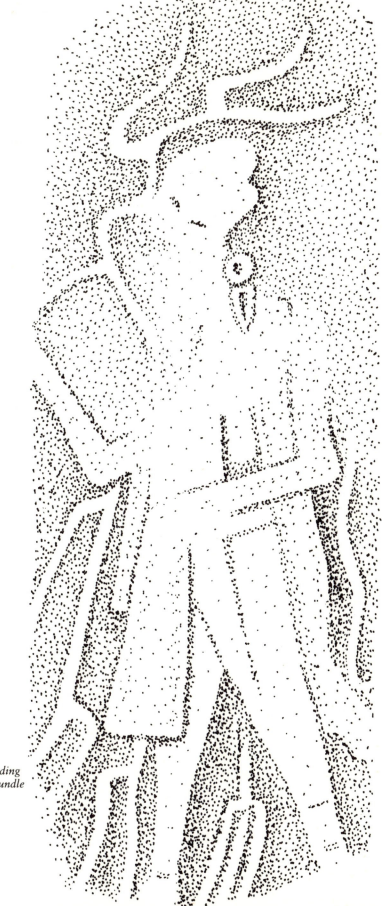

13 Monument 28, a highly
eroded stela depicting a standing
person possibly carrying a bundle
in the left arm. Ht 4 m.

stone. The flat upper surface of this large cylinder is uncarved, but is scarred by ploughing; one side has sustained damage, perhaps through mutilation.

The stela and its round altar are puzzling for they seem an anachronism. The combination of a ruler's portrait stela and a circular altar is common many hundreds of miles south and one thousand years later among the Classic Maya, but are unknown among the Olmec. Several occur at the site of Izapa near the Pacific coast in southern Mexico but are currently dated to the Late Formative period. [33] Because Chalcatzingo has cultural links to other frontier sites on the Pacific coast (see chapter 10), the ultimate solution to the anachronism may lie in a better understanding of those sites and their relationship to the heartland Olmec.

The implications of Monument 21, the stela featuring a female, are equally important and provide one possible clue to the nature of Chalcatzingo's relationship with the Gulf coast. Anthropological studies have shown that one way in which indigenous groups in many parts of the world strengthen

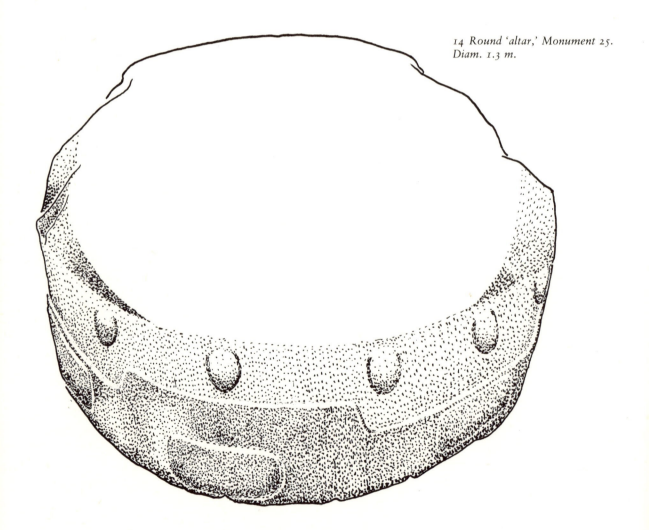

14 Round 'altar,' Monument 25. Diam. 1.3 m.

economic ties and alliances is through marriage. Because this is the only female depicted in the art of that period, and she occurs at a distant frontier site which we presume to have had important economic interactions with the Olmec heartland (see chapter 10), the woman of Monument 21 may represent the daughter of a Gulf coast ruler or leader who married into Chalcatzingo's ruling family to secure a long-distance relationship.[34] This is hypothetical, but there is little doubt that the woman had an important position and status at Chalcatzingo. Having assumed a role of considerable significance she was commemorated with her own monument. Only extremely powerful individuals received such treatment, and a marriage alliance makes more sense than many previous hypotheses (which are further discussed in chapter 10).

Until now this chapter has focused on platform architecture and stelae. However, a second type of important public area and monument was unearthed by excavations on Terrace 25, between the platforms of Terrace 15 and Terrace 25.

Because research priorities were directed toward residential structures, most monumental finds were purely fortuitous. Thus again, several flat stones barely exposed in a plough furrow caught the attention of co-director Raul Arana, who cleared away the topsoil and discovered several carved lines. Excavations soon disclosed that the stones were part of a row of large, faced, rectangular blocks which were ultimately seen to form a stone construction nearly 1 m tall that closely resembled the large monolithic 'tabletop altars' from the Olmec centers of San Lorenzo and La Venta.

plate 22

Rectangular in form, tabletop altars are so named because their characteristic upper ledge extends like a tabletop outward from the main body of the monument. They look like huge stone tables. At La Venta and San Lorenzo these so-called altars are monolithic, expertly carved from one massive piece of stone. Chalcatzingo's altar is curious, for although suitable boulders lie not far from Terrace 25, it is shorter than the Gulf coast altars of which it is obviously a copy and was manufactured out of large stone blocks carefully stacked together in a three-sided construction. Thus although not an exact duplicate of Olmec altars, it remains the first and only such altar discovered outside a Gulf coast center. Its presence at Chalcatzingo demonstrates the special relationship which existed between the Gulf coast and this highland center.

Gulf coast altars are characterized by a large arched niche in their front face. Within that niche, carved as part of the altar, is usually a high relief carving, a semi-statue, portraying a ruler. The symbolism is that which has already been described for the *El Rey* (Monument 1) relief, a cave entrance to the underworld with the seated person representing among various implied messages their access to the supernatural powers of the underworld, and in altars, their right to rule. To call these monolithic carvings altars is in fact probably incorrect. They are rulership-oriented in their iconography, and may actually have served as a ruler's throne (see chapter 9).[35]

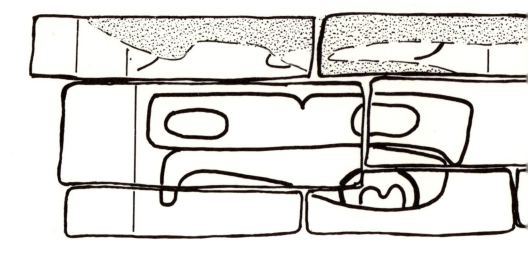

Monument 22, Chalcatzingo's 4-m-long altar, lacks the frontal niche. Instead, carved across the stones below the protruding tabletop ledge, are the eyes and undulating eyebrows of a supernatural earth monster. Such a creature is implicit on Gulf coast Olmec altars through the frontal niche; here it is explicit.

As the altar was being excavated we were puzzled because a section of one eye of the earth-monster face was uncarved. It soon became apparent that at sometime during its history the blocks forming the altar had been disassembled, perhaps to move the monument, or perhaps as an act of ritual destruction or mutilation. For whatever reason, it had been reassembled incorrectly (quite possibly on purpose). The stone containing the carving of the missing eye section had been reused in a different position, to form one sidewall on the altar, and replaced in its original location by a plain uncarved slab.

As excavations around the altar progressed, it was discovered that this Gulf coast-like monument sat at the south end of a slightly sunken patio area outlined on the west, south, and east sides by low stone walls. The altar itself faced north, and was flanked by stone benches which extended outwards along the south wall. The benches were stone slabs, each incorporating triangular-shaped niches with stones forming protruding eyes: faces which again symbolized the earth supernatural.

Beneath the earthen surface of the patio area were seventeen human burials. These were clearly an exception to the community's normal practice of burial beneath house floors (see chapter 6), indicating that the seventeen individuals interred might have had special status for which they were accorded burial in a separate precinct. Most of those buried within the patio were adults. Two

fig. 15

plates VII, 24

plate 30

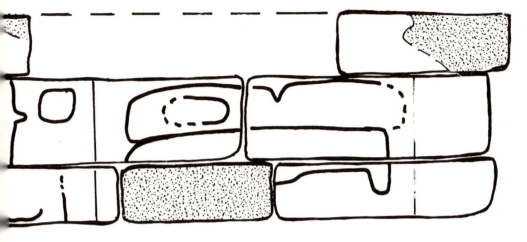

15 The carved earth-monster face covering the front of Monument 22, the tabletop altar, as discovered. Note the missing eye area on the right (shaded). L 4.4 m.

obviously important people had been interred at different times within the earthen core of the altar itself. One of those may have been the ruler who was in his lifetime associated with the altar.

Not all the individuals found beneath the patio necessarily died natural deaths. During the exploratory excavations of the altar the skeleton of an infant was found below the east front corner. That infant burial probably plate 31 represents a sacrifice made when the altar was constructed there. A pair of child burials at one corner of the patio also leads one to suggest something other than natural causes in order to explain the death of two small children of approximately the same age at a time so close that they were interred together. Finally, near the center of the patio, excavations uncovered a lone skull (adult) placed atop a ring of stones which surrounded a group of three ceramic bowls, one filled with red pigment.

The archaeology of the patio area and Terrace 25 is complex. A number of 'events' can be defined and placed in a general chronological order.[36] The earliest of them (after the construction of the terrace itself) was the building of a Barranca phase house in the same approximate location as the altar (which was later). Data on this house are meager, for all that survives is a minute fragment of house floor and a large subfloor refuse pit. An individual buried within the pit was associated with a stingray spine, an object linked with ritual blood-letting, and one so rare at the site that it suggests the individual may have been a high-ranked person.

Event two is the placement of the altar and patio during the Cantera phase. plate 23 Because the patio builders had dug down into the existing terrace surface, its plates 16–17 construction effectively destroyed most vestiges of the earlier Barranca phase house.

Event three is difficult to separate from event two because we cannot determine if any time at all elapsed between them, or to which event the altar's incorrect reassembly belongs. The third event represents the moment when the altar no longer served its original function and underwent ritual destruction. This was accomplished by hiding the carved earth-monster face behind a neatly laid pile of rectangular blocks taken from the tabletop upper surface; it was in that state when we excavated it. The majority of the burials found in Terrace 25 date to after event three, when the altar, with its carved face hidden, still sat exposed in the open patio.

plate 22

The two individuals interred within the altar clearly died after event two. Although impossible to prove, it is plausible that the death of the second individual may have precipitated event three, for as I shall discuss later, monument destruction appears directly related to a ruler's death. The patio burials could have been members of the ruling lineage, buried in the lineage precinct – the patio – near their deceased ancestor.

The importance of Terrace 25 did not end with event three and the burials. Later, to the south of the patio, a stone platform was built and a carved stela (Monument 23) erected. This is event four, and it indicates that the importance of the lineage continued.

In considering the data on major public architecture it is unfortunate that the current ceramic chronology cannot subdivide the Cantera phase into a series of much finer time segments. It is hoped that this will one day be achieved, for such a typology would enable us to reconstruct the sequence of construction of various Cantera structures, including the stone-faced platforms. At present we can only surmise that they were built at different times during that phase. To know more precisely in what sequence, and how they relate temporally to other events on the site, could elucidate a great deal more about such matters as land use and patterns of rulership.

6 Houses, burials, and social ranking

The public or elite area is focused on the upper terraces around Terrace 1. Residences were located on the many other terraces and on part of the unmodified hillside. As we have seen, Cantera phase house remains could usually be identified by the concentration of ceramic debris visible on the present-day ground surface. From the manner of distribution of those concentrations, and from test excavations, it became apparent that the Cantera phase settlement was not a tightly nucleated village. Each house stood well apart from its neighbors on a large field. The main function served by these big house plots was probably agricultural, with some food crops being grown there and supplemented by other crops planted on land away from the immediate village area.[37]

Nearly all that survives of the houses are their stone foundation walls. These demonstrate that Cantera phase houses at Chalcatzingo were about three times larger than any others known archaeologically from that period in Mexico. The average floor area encompassed by the foundation walls was slightly over 64 sq. m, which is twice the size of the one complete Barranca phase house uncovered by excavation. Smaller foundation lines within the residences, as well as some differential artifact distributions where ploughing had not totally destroyed the floors, suggest that partitions subdivided the houses into several large room units, each of which served one or more major activities.

Each house usually had both wide and narrow types of stone exterior-wall foundations. Back walls and both side walls were supported by wide foundations two to three stones across. The walls above the large foundations were apparently of sun-dried mud bricks; such bricks do not stand the ravages of time well and only a few heavily eroded examples were found. In contrast the foundations for front (entrance) walls of structures, and those for interior partitions, were only single rows of stones. The debris alongside them includes pieces of burned clay with impressions of thick plant stalks, an excellent indicator that the walls had been constructed of cane covered with a plaster-like coating of mud. No archaeological evidence for roofs or roof supports was found, but we surmise that they were made from a frame of poles covered with thatch.

The few undamaged areas of house floor found were of packed earth, sometimes built above a subfloor layer of small stones. Only one of the Cantera phase houses excavated had definite firepits in the floor. Most cooking appears to have been done on ceramic braziers. Those braziers and the foods exploited are discussed in the following chapter.

Food storage pits, so common at other sites of this period, were not found associated with Cantera phase houses. This need not mean they did not occur at the site, but is probably a reflection on the excavation strategy which concentrated on house interiors: external storage pits would simply have been missed.

Although the ruined condition of the house structures can be attributed in part to centuries of ploughing, we discovered that much of the damage was caused by their ancient residents, who had purposely destroyed and rebuilt them repeatedly in the same location possibly over several centuries.

plate 34

The jumble of subfloor foundation walls left by the many rebuildings is often quite complex. The destruction of the houses was carried out at least partially by burning, seen today by the fire-hardened chunks of cane-impressed mud plaster incorporated into the soil of house areas.

Some scholars have used evidence of burned houses as a sign of inter-village warfare, but such an explanation seems inappropriate here. The archaeological data suggest that much of the house, including the mud-brick walls, was dismantled prior to burning the more combustible portions. Cane and thatch are construction materials subject to deterioration and insect infestation and are also easily replaced. Mud bricks are harder to manufacture and it is logical that they were saved for reuse.

House destruction may have been motivated by the practical consideration of ridding the cane and thatch of vermin and the need simply to renew the more perishable materials, or by the desire to expand the house size. However, we cannot be certain that destruction was not carried out for deeper motives as well, such as at the death of the household head. Tiny pieces of broken jade ornaments occur in the soil and ash related to house destruction activities. These strongly hint that house destruction was accompanied by rituals involving the breakage of minor jade artifacts, and probably pottery as well.[38]

fig. 16

The house we have identified as belonging to a member of the elite (probably a chief) located on the south edge of Terrace 1, is identical to other Cantera phase houses in its construction, but is slightly larger in floor area (84 sq. m). It faced west onto a small (800 sq. m) courtyard. Two lesser structures, subdivided into several small rooms, faced onto the courtyard from its south side. When excavated, the courtyard itself proved to be very shallow, with the modern ploughzone resting almost on the sterile *tepetate*. A number of pieces of natural iron ore were found in the courtyard area and several had at least one side flattened through coarse grinding.

Artifacts manufactured from natural iron ores have been recovered at several Formative period sites. The most famous are the beautiful concave

16 *Plan of the foundation stones of the elite residential structure on Terrace 1.*

mirrors found at La Venta. Archaeological research at the village of San José Mogote, Oaxaca, disclosed artisans' areas where polished iron-ore mirrors had been manufactured along with other items. Utilizing specialized laboratory techniques, scientists have been able to match polished mirrors from San José Mogote as well as from other sites with naturally occurring ore bodies in the mountains near that site. From data such as these, archaeologists are able to match artifacts and sources, and to reconstruct patterns of exploitation of local raw materials and of trade and exchange of manufactured products.[39]

fig. 17

Polished iron-ore mirror fragments and a complete concave mirror were found during the Chalcatzingo research, but the laboratory analyses indicate that they are manufactured from ores of different composition from the ore pieces recovered in the courtyard. The coarse grinding on the courtyard samples suggests that they were being ground to produce red pigment for body painting, and not for the manufacture of mirror-like objects. Ore pieces, together with lumps of partially worked greenstone, were also recovered from within the two lesser courtyard structures, strongly implying that these were workshops. Craft practices of this scale are not present at other house areas, indicating that at Chalcatzingo such activities were controlled or carried out by a few elite individuals.

plate 26

Although human burials were sometimes found in non-residential contexts, such as the Terrace 25 patio, the majority of interments within the ancient

17 Grey ceramic duck vessel, found during excavation of the 'workshop' structure southeast of Terrace 1's elite residence. Estimated L. 15 cm.

village were beneath house floors. Most houses had six to eight burials, but the Terrace 1 elite residence yielded an astonishing total of thirty-eight. While many of those were similar in terms of associated mortuary goods or the embellishment of the grave itself to the burials in non-elite residences, others were far more elaborate.

Working on the assumption that a person's social rank, role, or wealth was reflected in the burial ritual and mortuary offerings they received, the site's Cantera phase burials were analyzed and given a general comparative ranking.[40] The elite and non-elite categories depend on visible criteria such as the elaborateness of the grave (labor expenditure), and on artifacts placed with the body at the time of interment (common, exotic, etc.).

Obviously there are some problems inherent in using mortuary criteria to hypothesize a person's social level. Perishable offerings may no longer be detectable. The age and sex of individuals might also have been socially significant, but in our skeletal sample most remains were too poorly preserved to allow those to be considered.

By using only grave goods to form a ranking, three basic levels can be differentiated. The simplest level is defined by the lack of any ceramic vessels or other major artifacts within the grave. Thirty-five percent of the Cantera phase burials fell within this category. Certainly more numerous are the burials found with one ceramic vessel or more, for this second level constitutes almost sixty percent of the total sample. No readily apparent relationship has yet been detected between the quantity of vessels received and ranking. In fact, some of the most elaborate graves have few pots.

The third and highest level is composed of burials containing jade and other greenstone ornaments (with or without ceramic vessels), on the assumption

plates 18, 35

plate 29

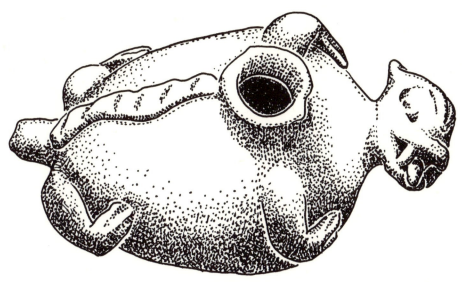

18 Ceramic dog vessel found in a crypt grave beneath the elite residence. L. 17 cm.

that jade artifacts were rare and highly valued. Here, not every ornament was of equal importance. Some individuals may have had only one greenstone bead, while others had several different jade articles of far more complex and difficult workmanship.

Three different grave categories, based on effort required and embellishment, can also be defined. The most basic grave is a simple unadorned pit into which the deceased was placed, and nearly eighty percent of graves were of that type. The second category, perhaps not significantly different from the first, consists of grave pits in which several stones have been placed at some section of the body (head, midsection, etc.). Ten percent of graves were of that type.

plate 32

The remaining eleven percent of graves demonstrate a greater labor investment, for they consist of stone crypts, and burials covered with a large amount of stones. The looted tomb found atop the large earthen platform mound is an example of this type. Stone crypts (the majority of this category) were constructed by lining the grave pit with small slabs of stone placed in an upright position to form a box-like construction around the interment. This box was normally capped with additional stone slabs.

A total of fourteen crypt graves were found, half of them beneath the floor of the elite residence, the only house to contain this special grave type. Two others were found near the earthen platform's looted tomb, and the remainder were beneath the patio associated with the altar on Terrace 25. Crypt burials appear to have been restricted to the society's most important individuals, for there is a strong correlation between crypt graves and jade offerings.

fig. 18

Two of Chalcatzingo's most 'Olmec' artifacts were recovered from a pair of superimposed crypt graves from the elite residence. One crypt, just at plates 25, 27

fig. 19, plate XIV

ploughzone depth and thus heavily damaged, contained Monument 17, a stone head broken off a statue, the rest of which was not found. Directly beneath the ploughzone crypt was a second. It contained an anthropomorphic greenstone figurine, similar to those from La Venta, but manufactured from stone of lower quality. The crypt pairing was apparently intentional, and could represent the burials of a ruler and his wife, or other individuals with significant ties to the Olmec heartland.

Among the jade artifacts found with other crypt burials, two 'levels' of jade offering can be differentiated. The two interments richest in jade were found atop the village's main public structure, the large earthen platform mound. Both individuals were buried within their crypt graves wearing a significant amount of jade ornaments. One wore a pair of jade earspools, a necklace of plate XIII forty-nine beads, a pelvic string of eight beads, and had a small greenstone adze placed on the chest. The second was equally richly adorned and further included shell insets in the jade earspools, ninety-four tiny square wafers of turquoise from a mosaic whose backing had long since disintegrated, and a plate 26 concave hematite mirror. That mirror is the first ever recovered with a burial, and its positioning shows it had been worn as a pectoral at the time of interment.

In contrast, none of the individuals buried beneath the elite house had actually worn the jade found with them. It generally consisted of pieces of broken objects such as earspools and awl-like perforators. From this it appears that only the most highly ranked members of the society were accorded a burial in which jade jewelry was worn. Few members of the society were apparently able to obtain that imported luxury item, and even fewer could afford to take it with them at death, for to be buried with jade meant that the precious items were permanently removed from circulation. Thus for the archaeologist the jade found with those burials has served as a valuable marker of ancient wealth and social rank. It can be seen that only a few members of the society had the ability to be interred wearing abundant jade jewelry; indeed, most of the elite received only a few broken pieces or no jade at all.

While it is probable that the vessels found in graves functioned in some manner in the burial ritual, there are few clues to their use. Some perhaps held liquids or perishable foods, while others had purely symbolic importance. The only vessel type to which we can attribute a role is the double-loop-handled censer, a form which in the field and lab received the informal designation of plate 38 'Easter baskets.'

The flat interior bases of the censers are blackened where a substance such as copal incense was burned. The resin of the copal tree is still widely used today in Mexico and Guatemala, including in burial rituals. Such censers occur with about ten percent of Chalcatzingo's burials, including crypt graves. It is in those contexts that their function is reaffirmed. In contrast to regular mortuary vessels, which always occur within the closed stone crypts, double-loop-handled censers are usually found beside or atop the crypt stones. That

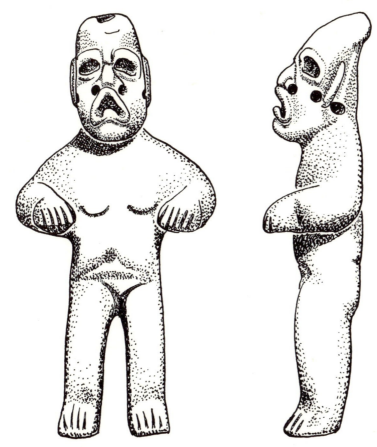

19 Werejaguar figurine recovered from a crypt burial beneath the floor of the elite residence on Terrace 1. Ht 11 cm.

positioning suggests that the censers were added to the grave at the end of the ritual, just prior to it being refilled with soil.

Although pottery offerings are generally poor markers of social rank, one exception stands out. Several crypt graves contained an unassuming combination of vessels: a small jar sitting inside a small shallow dish. Both vessels are always plain, with no decoration, are only half as large as most mortuary pottery, yet together seem to be markers of elite rank. Importantly, this same combination was found in an elite grave at the Gulf coast Olmec site of La Venta, confirming its value as a status marker.[41]

The burial data, then, suggest that certain markers such as crypt graves, jade and greenstone artifacts, and shallow bowls holding miniature jars, can be used individually and collectively to distinguish highly ranked individuals. These we refer to here as elite. Only one residence on the site contains burials with those traits, and for that reason we have identified it as an elite residence.

plate 39

plate 33

Burials beneath the floors of other houses always lacked elite traits.

Having presented the data on residential and public structures in this and the previous chapter, the Cantera phase community at Chalcatzingo becomes clearer. The size of the population of the village can only be estimated, however, and there are nearly as many means and formulas for doing so as there are scholars working on the topic. One method frequently used in surface reconnaissance in central Mexico combines the spatial extent of surface sherd scatter (site size) and the density with which the pottery pieces from a particular period cover the ground.[42] The underlying assumption is that more broken pottery indicates a greater population. The estimate given in chapter 4 for the small Barranca phase village at Chalcatzingo was calculated using that method.[43] The same technique would produce an estimate for the large Cantera phase village of between 433 and 1081 persons.

However, I am reasonably sure that there were approximately twenty Cantera phase houses on the main site and closely adjacent fields, and that provides a different way of estimating population. The number of people occupying a house at a particular time must be estimated using house-floor area, and occupant density within a house varies from society to society throughout the world, so there is no completely satisfactory and universal formula. One frequently used, and just as frequently criticized, depends on a figure of 10 sq. m of floor area per person. The average Cantera phase dwelling had 64 sq. m of floor area, yielding an estimate of 6–7 inhabitants. That estimate may of course be too low or too high. Since much smaller dwellings around the world are known to house a basic nuclear family of 4 or 5 persons (husband, wife and offspring), it is possible that Chalcatzingo's larger houses were residences for extended families (several generations of one family).

On the other hand, estimates based on a structure's floor area assume that the entire structure served residential purposes. It is entirely possible that at Chalcatzingo some rooms of the houses had been used for the storage of crops or other items. In such a case, the 6–7 person estimate may be somewhat high.

Combining the estimated number of houses in the main site area (20) with a figure of 7 persons per residence yields a population estimate for the Cantera phase of only 140, a figure far below the figure based on surface data. The number seems very low in the light of Chalcatzingo's importance as a regional center. On the other hand the estimate may be more correct than 433–1083, for there are many drawbacks to using purely surface-sherd distributions to calculate population. It is possible that archaeologists tend to overestimate populations of early farming societies because their only models for comparison are historical, a time of far greater world populations.

Chalcatzingo's importance need not necessarilly have depended on a large populace. The function of the settlement and the rank of the persons residing there are far more significant factors in determining a site's regional and inter-regional status than the quantity of its inhabitants. Chalcatzingo was no exception.

7 Reconstructing daily life

One of the hardest tasks facing an archaeologist is to put some cultural 'flesh' onto the bare data skeleton which they excavate. From our excavations we gained some idea of house forms and the expansion of the settlement over several centuries, and from the subfloor burials we have managed to develop a hypothetical model of social ranking. But, what aspects of daily life can be reconstructed from the artifacts found?

Although the soil excavated from each house was carefully sifted – and samples subjected to a process known as floatation in an effort to recover seeds or other organic remains which might provide an idea of the diet – preservation was very poor and no good botanical remains were uncovered. However, it is possible to infer that the basic maize-beans-squash triumvirate, traditional for several thousand years in Mesoamerica and found archaeologically elsewhere at this period, was also consumed here.

Good evidence of this lies in the processing tools common in our excavations. These are the *manos* (hand stones) and *metates* (querns) nearly identical to those still used to grind maize kernels into a paste or flour for use in foodstuffs such as *tamales*, *tortillas*, and as a gruel-like drink, *atole*. While most tools of this kind recovered were worn from the longitudinal grinding required for maize processing, a few mortar and pestle-like stones were probably used for crushing and pounding seeds and nuts collected wild on the hillside and in the unoccupied areas surrounding the village.

All these grinding or pounding stones are made of igneous rock – a local granodiorite gathered from around the base of the cliff, and from basalt and other igneous river-rounded cobbles brought from the rocky bed of the Amatzinac River. The people of Chalcatzingo never lacked stone for grinding tools or for house construction.

Other evidence documenting an important foodstuff is found with the site's famed bas-relief carvings. Three of the carvings near *El Rey* depict very realistic squash plants, one showing incipient fruit. The realism of the carving plate 12 leaves no doubt from the morphology of the plants that squash are being represented (see chapter 8).

The villagers at Chalcatzingo were not vegetarians, as the bones in every house excavation showed. It is clear that hunting was carried out in two nearby ecological zones. Deer were hunted in the valley woodlands and hills to the north and east of the village, while cottontail rabbits from the drier grasslands to the south were also popular. Although complete skeletons of two immature peccaries (wild pigs) were found near one house structure, no peccary bones were recovered from domestic garbage. Their age and unbutchered condition suggest the peccaries were killed for ritual rather than gastronomic purposes.

Only a few bird bones were recovered, perhaps because they are more delicate and survived less well. Those found include minor quantities of turkey, duck, hawk, and parrot. The most abundant animal in the diet was the dog. Chalcatzingo is fairly unusual in the highlands in that dog remains predominate over those of deer and rabbit, a pattern more typical of tropical lowland areas, including the Gulf coast.[44]

One of the many laboratory analyses carried out in conjunction with the project was the determination of the strontium content in the bones of a large sample of Chalcatzingo's human burials. In theory, humans who consume meat regularly in their diet will have a smaller percentage of bone strontium than individuals who regularly eat a diet heavy in vegetables. In antiquity it was also frequently the case that through social and other constraints, elite and nobility ate more meat than non-elite. The analysis of Chalcatzingo's skeletal material revealed that a great deal of variation existed in the diets of both elite and non-elite individuals (as classified by criteria discussed in chapter 6). However, taken as a group, the elite had less bone strontium, meaning that their diets were indeed more abundant in meat.[45]

As previously mentioned, cooking was usually carried out on special ceramic braziers rather than over open fires. Most ceramic braziers were shaped like squat hourglasses and averaged about 30 cm in diameter. Each *fig. 20* usually had three wide prongs which projected upward and slightly inward from the upper rim to support a vessel above charcoal held in the brazier.

While some of those supporting prongs are plain, many are in the form of animal heads, and others seem to depict supernatural creatures. Among the *plate 41* animals depicted are canines and peccaries. Nearly all the prongs are smudged at the point where they supported the cooking pots, for such a contact point would have received less oxygen during the heating.

Brazier supports of that type have not been reported from Formative period sites elsewhere in central Mexico, but have been recovered in Oaxaca and on the Gulf coast.[46] The braziers are only one of many non-local traits which demonstrate that while much of the site's material culture was indigenous to the highland region, other traits were extra-regional in origin.

The project laboratory estimates that over one million pottery sherds were recovered during the course of the excavations, and these were studied and analyzed with a number of goals in mind. Any differentiation of pottery into ritual and non-ritual categories would have been purely subjective and was not attempted. Seldom were vessels found in contexts which were unquestionably

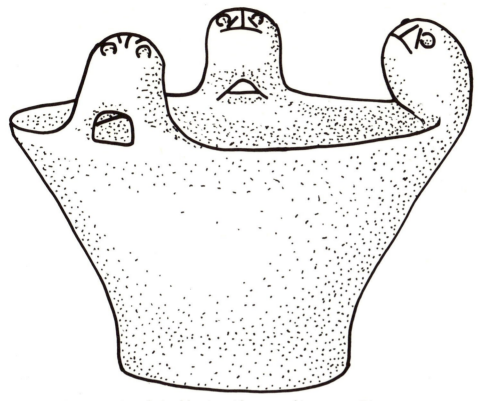

20 Reconstruction of tripod brazier with zoomorphic supports. Diam. c. 30 cm.

ritual. Even in those rare instances, the pottery was seldom distinguishable from that found in household or burial contexts. In other words, almost all the pottery could have served a utilitarian function.

Clearly, undecorated pottery is most easily classifiable as utilitarian, although there are pitfalls in assuming even this. It should be recalled that the small pots placed in shallow bowls are apparently important elite markers of equal status to jade and crypts. Yet they are undecorated, and on their own they are undistinctive.

Even decorated pottery may have had other than ritual functions. Research at Early Formative period settlements in the Valley of Oaxaca has determined that some so-called Olmec decorative motifs appear to have been social markers used by different segments of a village as lineage or clan identifiers, rather than signifying any relationship with Gulf coast Olmec. The social value and meaning of various decorative elements on pottery vessels is a topic requiring more study from archaeologists.[47]

A good deal of Chalcatzingo's Early Formative pottery is heavily decorated with symbolic motifs which dominate the vessels, for probably the same social reasons as found among Valley of Oaxaca villages. However, Middle

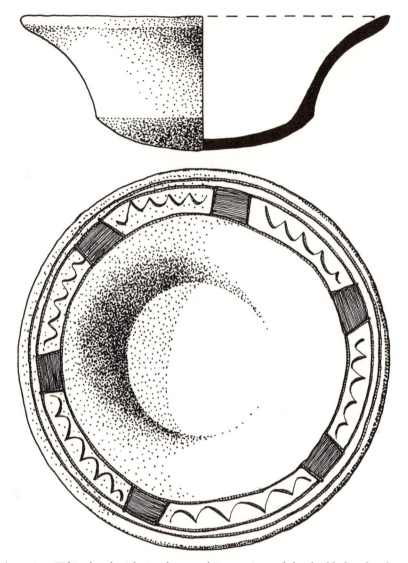

21 Amatzinac White bowl with rim decorated in a variant of the double-line-break motif. Diam. 25 cm.

Formative pottery designs are far more subtle, not only at Chalcatzingo, but throughout Mesoamerica. This may imply that by that time the overt belief system was expressed in other mediums or via rituals which left little or no archaeological remains. It may imply too that certain ideas earlier expressed publicly on pottery had since moved into the domain of religious specialists. One might also suggest that it was no longer important to communicate those earlier ideas.

The most common vessel at Chalcatzingo during the Middle Formative period shared its popularity with much of Mexico at that time. This was a

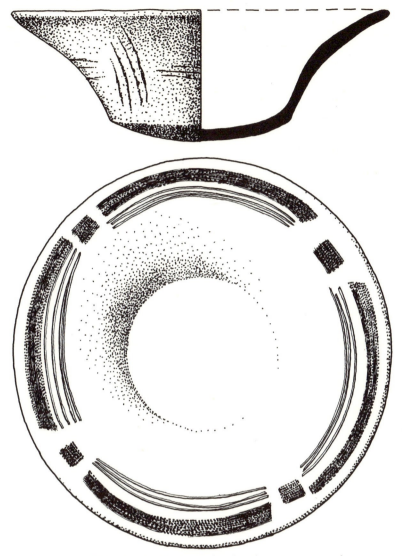

22 Amatzinac White bowl with double-line-break variant as rim decoration.
Diam. 26 cm.

white bowl with outcurving sides and a slightly rounded bottom. The center interior of the bowl was sometimes decorated with an incised design, and the rim almost always with the motif identified in chapter 3 as the 'double-line-break.' Such bowls are excellent markers for this period even though some variation occurs over time.[48]

figs 21–2, plate 36

This bowl form and decoration were popular in a large region of Mesoamerica, but represent here a locally manufactured version of a widespread style, rather than a trade ware emanating from a particular region. Despite claims to the contrary, the origin area of the style remains to be determined. Although there are some minor regional variations to white wares with the double-line-break motif, potters everywhere appear to have followed the same basic steps of production. The form was hand modeled, perhaps using a ceramic mould (the ceramic potter's wheel was not used in ancient Mesoamerica), from the same clay used in manufacturing nearly all locally made vessels, ritual or utilitarian. After the vessel had dried it was then given a thin slip of white clay. Once that coating had dried, a sharpened tool was used to incise the designs on the vessel by scratching through the white layer. The vessel was then fired in an oxidizing (non-blackening) atmosphere. When it had been removed from the kiln and had cooled, the potter often gave a shine to its white surface by burnishing the vessel with a hard smooth object such as a polished pebble or even a piece of maize stalk.

An important question, and unfortunately one which remains to be investigated throughout Mesoamerica, is the type of clay used for the nearly ubiquitous white slip. Very few clays will fire a pure white. Several tests carried out both in the field and in the laboratory indicate that at Chalcatzingo the white slip is kaolin, a clay common in fine dinnerware today. A small number of white sherds from several other sites outside the region have been tested with the same results. Because kaolin-clay sources are apparently relatively rare in Mesoamerica, it is possible that this raw material was traded from source areas to other regions. It may not be coincidental that Chalcatzingo is situated very near to one of the oldest known kaolin sources in central Mexico.[49]

plate 37

A surprising element in Chalcatzingo's Cantera phase ceramic inventory is its polychrome pottery, the earliest yet known in Mexico. The most common vessel form is a shallow bowl made of clay local to the Chalcatzingo area. The rims of these bowls are usually decorated with a band of red paint, while the exterior of the bowl has simple but unusual designs painted in red, brown, orange, and black. Though white pottery decorated with simple red-painted designs is known both at Chalcatzingo and sites in the Basin of Mexico, the addition of other colors to create polychrome motifs is new and different. However, such polychrome pottery may not be unique to Chalcatzingo. During the 1966 excavations at a small Middle Formative site in west-central Morelos, Las Juntas, I found a small number of nearly identical polychrome sherds. It is impossible to tell at this stage whether Chalcatzingo was the source and Las Juntas the recipient, or whether a third site is the source. Mineralogical analyses of the polychrome sherds recovered at Chalcatzingo indicate that the ware was manufactured locally and not imported from another area, but further work remains to be done on this unique pottery type.

figs 23–4

A common ware at the site, Peralta Orange, occurs both as wide bowls with sharply angular sides and as round storage or water jars with relatively narrow necks. The color of the vessels comes from a heavy orange slip applied so as to create a frequently streaky appearance. The pots are often decorated on their exterior surfaces by triangular punctations in simple linear arrangements.

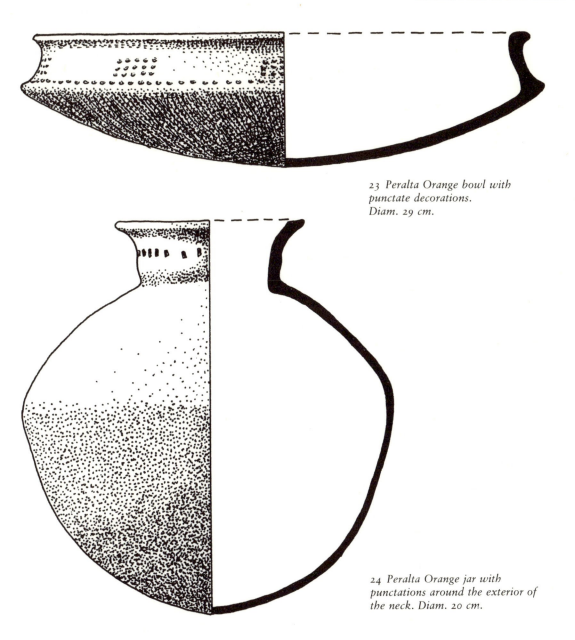

23 Peralta Orange bowl with
punctate decorations.
Diam. 29 cm.

24 Peralta Orange jar with
punctations around the exterior of
the neck. Diam. 20 cm.

Although made from local clay and very common at the site and throughout
the valley, Peralta Orange is not found at other central Mexican sites. It thus
belongs to the small but important complex of artifacts distinctive to
Chalcatzingo and affiliated sites in the Amatzinac valley.

As part of our research, the project ceramicist traveled to the Smithsonian
Institution in Washington DC, to examine ceramics recovered in the earlier
excavations at the Olmec sites of La Venta and Tres Zapotes, and now in
storage there. Pottery similar to Peralta Orange was found in those collections,

possessing both the punctate decorations and several peculiar bottle-neck forms.[50]

Orange ceramics similar in color and treatment to both Peralta Orange and the Gulf coast orange ware is also found at Middle (and Late) Formative period sites in the Maya area, to the south of the Gulf coast. It is possible that the orange ceramics in the Olmec heartland represent influences emanating from those areas further to the south, and that via the Gulf coast some 'southern influences' arrived at Chalcatzingo.[51]

A number of other generalized 'southern' traits occur in the site's ceramic inventory. Three-pronged cooking braziers – although without hollow zoomorphic prongs – occur in Middle and Late Formative assemblages in Guatemala. Too, the plate-like ceramics with roughened bottoms found at Chalcatzingo are similar to *tortilla* griddles used by later Mesoamerican peoples and to those which are made and sold for the same purpose today. Although previously unreported for the Middle Formative period in central Mexico, similar griddle-like forms have been found at Yarumela in central Honduras, and at Chalchuapa, El Salvador, in deposits as old or older than those at Chalcatzingo. Perhaps not coincidentally, Chalchuapa, like Chalcatzingo, has Olmec-style rock carvings.[52]

Whether these *comal*-like platters served the same function at Formative period Chalcatzingo as they do today for making *tortillas* is a matter of conjecture and in need of further testing. Maize must be soaked in lime water to soften it properly for grinding into the dough (*masa*) used for *tortillas*. Thus, lime is required, and there is excellent evidence of lime-making and storage at the site. Its ultimate use is unknown.

During the excavation of an unusual feature at the southwest corner of the site, a deposit of processed lime was uncovered which extended over an area of approximately 160 sq. m and had a maximum thickness of about 50 cm. There was a 'structure' formed by three rows of large stones set vertically in the soil and spaced a few meters apart to create a large rectangle with one open side. Much of the lime deposit was within the rectangular area but also ran slightly uphill.

The artifact assemblage from this area was not substantially different from that of normal house structures, except for several small ceramic banana-shaped objects. These unusual artifacts show signs of wear along their sides as if they functioned for smoothing or polishing concave objects such as the unfired interiors of pottery vessels. If these clay banana-like objects are potter's tools, the 'structure' may be a potter's workshop. But the lime deposit here is perplexing since lime does not seem to serve a function in ceramic manufacturing and is certainly not the color medium for Chalcatzingo's white wares.

The discovery of processed lime demonstrates that the technology of lime manufacture was known at the site even though the lime was not used for plaster as it was at San José Mogote, Oaxaca.[53] The technology requires that raw limestone be burned in above-ground or subsurface kilns. Several later lime kilns, dating to *c.* A D 800, were found during our Chalcatzingo research, but no earlier lime kilns were discovered. Limestone outcrops occur only a few miles southwest of Chalcatzingo, along the west side of the valley.

plate 40

Just as evidence of lime kilns is missing, so too is any sign of kilns for firing ceramics. But the sampling techniques used for deciding where to excavate may have negatively biased the chances for finding such areas. In any future exploration of the site a magnetometer could be used to locate burned areas (as well as buried structures) without the expense of excavations.

Although ceramic sherds constitute over ninety-nine percent of the finds, a variety of minor artifacts provide equally valuable insights. These include elite jade items, simple jewelry of baked clay, objects for body decoration, whistles, flutes, and, of course, figurines. The latter will be considered here first, for their abundance indicates that they were important in the belief system of Chalcatzingo's inhabitants.

Because these excavations were the largest ever carried out at a Formative period site in highland central Mexico, the sample from each artifact category is likewise the greatest to date. The figurine sample consists of over 4000 arm, leg, body, and head pieces, of both anthropomorphic and zoomorphic representations. Among the anthropomorphic figurine fragments – the vast majority of the sample – it is the heads and their great variability that attract attention.

Chalcatzingo's figurine heads are nearly identical to those found at sites in the Valley of Mexico. They were analyzed according to the basic classification established for that region by George Vaillant in his research and publications nearly fifty years ago. That typology used facial shape and features as the distinguishing factors of the various figurine head types. He labeled his dozen types with the letters A through L. His types C and D exhibited enough internal variation that Vaillant further subdivided them with numerical suffixes.[54]

plates 50–2

Archaeologists realize the chronological value of Vaillant's typology, and see some figurines as good general markers. In the recently revised chronology of the central Mexican Formative period, D1- and D2-type figurine heads ('pretty-lady figurines') and K types are common during the Early Formative, while the Middle Formative period is principally characterized by B, C2, C3, and C5 types – and at Chalcatzingo by C8 heads as well.

During the Early Formative period in central Mexico, figurines are found associated with burials as well as in domestic contexts. By the Middle Formative they were seldom placed in graves, and their abundance around residential areas suggests their probable use in household rituals. Figurine bodies frequently emphasize female sexual characteristics, and exhibit particularly wide thighs. For this reason, some archaeologists have hypothesized that figurines functioned in fertility rites, although because they

25 *Seated figurine wearing a bird-like headdress which continues down the back. The figurine is an Amatzinac valley variant of a central Mexican C type figurine. Ht 9 cm.*

are also found in areas away from houses, they might have been left in the agricultural fields to insure good crops.

Whereas in some cases the archaeologist can turn to the written reports of early Spanish settlers of Mexico to shed light on questions of artifact function, very little documentary evidence exists for conquest-period figurine use. Padre Durán describes figurines strung by cords in Aztec corn fields, and also records that all Aztec houses had a small shrine with figurines, as did some Maya homes.[55] However, it is unclear if a direct analogy can be made, for there is no mention in the documents of the purposeful breakage of figurines, such as is found in our site. From various archaeological contexts it is clear that the breakages date from the figurines' period of use. In fact, breakage was probably the action that terminated a figurine's social function.

At the time of the Spanish conquest, many of the figurines used in Aztec society were merely small clay representations of the Aztec deities also depicted on large stone monuments. But no such correlation exists for Formative period figurines, and there is no evidence that concepts of formal anthropomorphic deities were part of the belief system of early agricultural societies. What then did figurines represent and what role did they fulfill in these societies?[56]

One particularly significant discovery has been made concerning Chalcatzingo's wealth of excavated figurines. Most of the figurines of this

period and area are generalized human representations. The B and C types of   *fig. 25*
the Middle Formative are typical of this. Their crude faces are only rough
approximations of human anatomy. An exception is the C8 figurine head type,
usually very rare and thus of only minor comparative value. However at
Chalcatzingo they are the most abundant of the types.

The facial modeling and attention given to facial details on C8 figurines sets
them apart from other types. They appear to be representations of specific
individuals. As these C8 figurines were studied it became clear that within the
large sample at least twenty different individuals could be identified. Each had
a specific headdress form which in turn correlated with the distinct facial
features. Each figurine 'individual' has been given an identification letter

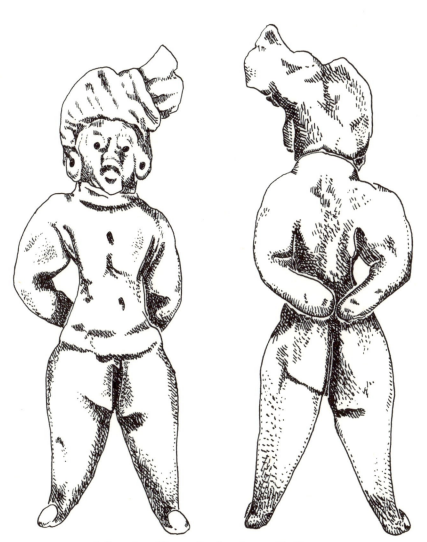

26 *Complete C8 type figurine, Person M. Ht 15 cm.*

plates 53–8
fig. 26

(Person A, Person B, etc.). Among the many C8 figurines, a number of heads (and in some instances they are part of complete figurines) of each 'person' occur.

A convincing argument can be made for the C8 figurine 'persons' to be seen as portraits of rulers, or perhaps the headmen of elite lineages at the site. The rarity or absence of such figurines at most other sites in central Mexico is highly significant. It suggests that C8 figurines are a phenomenon of Chalcatzingo, a special type of figurine reflecting the special nature of this Middle Formative settlement. As we discussed in chapter 5, chiefly portraiture in monuments was equally important at the site. Together, the personification of certain individuals in monuments and figurines has led to the discovery of an important belief theme, the cult of the revered ancestor or ruler.[57] Because most portrait monuments have been mutilated, it is difficult to match these with the type-C8 clay figurines, but one good correspondence has been found. A C8 figurine type we have labeled Person D represents an old man with puffy

plate 59

facial features who wears a pointed headdress. The identical features are depicted on Monument 10, the final monument discussed in chapter 8.

plate 60

Although the vast majority of figurines are anthropomorphic, animal figurines are also present. Some are easily identifiable as animals native to the

plates 61–3

region, such as squirrels, peccaries, opossums, and dogs. Among the birds, there are owls, turkeys, and ducks which are also local to central Mexico, although ducks would have been far more common around the lake in the Basin of Mexico than in the Amatzinac valley. Monkey-figurine heads depict an animal clearly foreign to the area. Few animal-figurine bodies were found, and there is evidence suggesting some of the animal-figurine heads came from hollow whistles.

The whistles found may have been used in rituals or simply as musical instruments. A ritual use is most plausible because whistles were usually made in a limited set of animal forms, some of which closely replicate whistles recovered years earlier in excavations at the Gulf coast site of Tres Zapotes.[58] Much of Chalcatzingo's Gulf coast artifact similarities occur in ritual and elite items, and whistles appear no different in that respect.

Many of the artifacts identified here as whistles are perhaps better defined as two- and three-toned ocarinas. Most are simply a hollow egg-shaped clay chamber to which a simple mouthpiece and a few basic features, including an animal's head, were appended. In whistles depicting birds, for instance, the

fig. 27, plate 64

oval chamber was the bird's body, the mouthpiece represented the tail, while tiny wings and the bird's head completed the rudimentary figure. In some monkey and opossum whistles the egg-shaped chamber does not form the body but is instead held on the animal's shoulders.

Only two whistles with human features were found, both very similar in construction and both unusual. Each is a simple human head, about 6 cm long, with puffy hollow cheeks, and holes above the cheeks for eyes. Some scholars

plate 65

have referred to such heads as the 'fat god.' These are two-toned whistles, for

The setting

1   The Amatzinac River valley north of Chalcatzingo. The Cerro Delgado is in the right foreground, the Cerro Jantetelco in the right center, and Popocatepetl volcano in the background. The deep *barranca* (gorge) of the river can be seen cutting down the valley. The village of Chalcatzingo is in the left center.

2   Aerial view of the Chalcatzingo area, with north to the left. The modern village can be seen at the lower left, near the river *barranca* which cuts diagonally across the picture. The site lies in the center, just below the hills (Cerro Delgado at left center, and the more massive Cerro Chalcatzingo at right center).

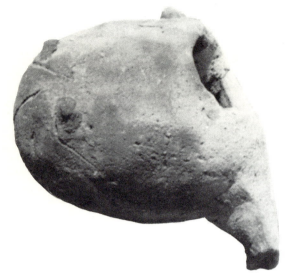

41 Tripod brazier prongs in zoomorphic forms. L. *c.* 13.5 cm.

Small finds

42 Solid disk earspools, Cantera phase. Diam. of central disk 2.3 cm.

43 Fragments of 'roller seals,' probably for decorating the human body. Ht *c.* 5 cm.

44 Ground sherd disks: unperforated, semi-perforated, and perforated. Probably for use in a game such as *patolli*. Upper row are made from Amatzinac White sherds. Diam. of upper left disk *c.* 4 cm.

45 A stingray spine probably used for ritual blood-letting. L. 6 cm.

46 Obsidian blood-letting needles. Longest, 6 cm.

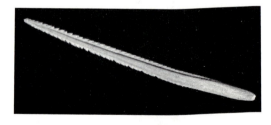

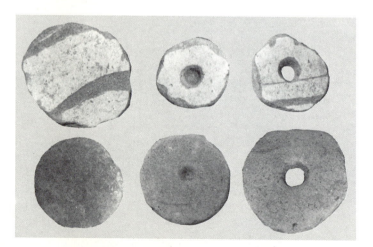

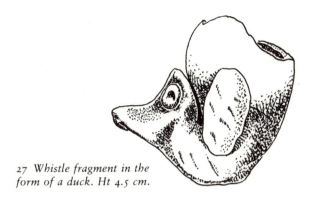

27 Whistle fragment in the form of a duck. Ht 4.5 cm.

each cheek is a sound chamber. The whistles are blown from the forehead area into the eyes, which are the inlets to the chambers.

Jade objects for elite personal adornment were briefly mentioned in the discussion of burials and social ranking. The use of such jewelry was restricted to a small segment of society, both in life and death. It is important to understand that such green stones were the most valued and revered substance in ancient Mesoamerica precisely because they were not abundant, and were a major commodity in the trade and exchange networks. Only one source of real nephrite jade is known today in Mesoamerica, and it is located in the Motagua valley of Guatemala, far to the south of the Gulf coast and Chalcatzingo. A second nephrite source may exist near Acatlan in Puebla, situated in the central highlands near Chalcatzingo, but its exact location has yet to be found. Lesser-quality green stones such as serpentine occur in the rugged mountains extending the length of Mesoamerica's Pacific coast. Some of the green stone used in ornaments at Chalcatzingo came from sources in the mountains of the state of Guerrero to the west.[59]

Many of the jade and greenstone artifacts arrived at the site already manufactured. However, some workshop debris, such as cut serpentine fragments and the cores from hollow drilling, indicate that a small jewelry industry operated in the structures adjacent to the elite residence on Terrace 1 (see chapter 6). The cores are produced by one of the two methods used to perforate holes in beads and other stone artifacts. The most common technique was conical drilling, in which a tapered drill (of unknown material) and an abrasive were used to bore a conical hole in an object. The resulting perforation is wide on one side and tiny on the other. On thicker objects, such as spherical beads, conical holes were bored from each side, meeting (the craftsman hoped) in the middle, creating an hourglass-shaped perforation.

A completely different drilling technique was used for holes of a greater diameter, and was also employed at a later period to hollow out the interiors of stone vessels. This apparently involved a hollow reed, an abrasive such as fine sand, and a great deal of patience. The reed tip was dipped in abrasive and slowly rotated, creating a circular cut which got deeper and deeper as the

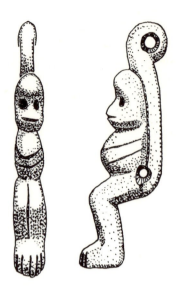

28 Jade pendant in the form of a spider monkey. Ht 6.5 cm.

drilling progressed. The result was eventually a cylindrical hole in the object and a cylindrical stone core in the interior of the hollow reed drill. These cores were discarded and when found by the archaeologist provide testimony to that workshop activity.

The majority of Chalcatzingo's jade and greenstone ornaments occur either as earspools, pendants, or beads. The earspools are circular in form and would have fitted into stretched openings in the earlobe. Two styles of earspools were found. One is thick with flaring sides and was found with elite burials. Those of the second style are very thin, tubular, and extremely delicate. None of the second type were found intact or in association with burials, but came from the fill comprising subfloors of both elite and non-elite residences. This is something of a puzzle, for it suggests that the thin earspools could be 'sacrificed' in the rituals performed at a residence's destruction, and that those who had used them were denied them at burial.

plate XIII

Beads and pendants were far more common ornaments. Most beads recovered were simple spheres or ovoids, but some tubular ones were also found, which may not all have functioned just as ornaments. Recent evidence indicates that hallucinogenic snuff was ritually used by a number of Formative period societies, and that some long tubular jade beads as well as long bird-bone beads functioned as snuff tubes.[60] Although hallucinogens continued to play an important part in Mesoamerican rituals up to the Spanish conquest, snuff use may have died out long before then.

Pendants were usually relatively simple, taking the form of animal fangs or small hollow hemispheres. Several T-shaped pendants similar to those recovered in archaeological excavations at Gulf coast Olmec centers were found, another trait linking Chalcatzingo to that area. The most elaborate of the pendants was a small jade monkey, an animal found in the tropical forests of the Gulf coast.

fig. 28

Only one whole greenstone figurine was found, in a crypt burial beneath the elite residence (see chapters 6 and 10). Several greenstone 'celts' were also recovered, but most appear to have been functional cutting implements, unlike the celts from La Venta, some of which were engraved, and most of which seem to have served ritual purposes. No La Venta-like celt caches were uncovered at Chalcatzingo.[61]

The non-elite at the site were not without objects of personal adornment, for clay beads, pendants, and earspools were found. The earspools, interestingly, are the most abundant of the clay ornaments, and are unlike their greenstone counterparts. Clay earspools are thick circular disks with slightly concave sides. They average about 2.5 cm in diameter and 13 mm in thickness. Nearly all lack incised or painted decorations. Earspools of this type have not been reported from Olmec sites, but were recovered by Vaillant at the Late Formative site of Ticoman in the Basin of Mexico.[62] Chalcatzingo's are slightly earlier than those from Ticoman and should be considered as a highland culture trait. It is undoubtedly not coincidental that it is non-elite, non-ritual artifacts which have the strongest central Mexican cultural affiliations.

plate 42

Both elite and non-elite members of the society at Chalcatzingo decorated their bodies with painted designs. Two different types of evidence lead to that conclusion. Faint traces of red and yellow designs can occasionally be seen on the site's figurines, and there is no reason to suspect that those do not reflect body painting on actual people. Designs could easily have been applied with the flat and cylindrical 'seals' recovered in both non-elite and elite contexts. Powdered red pigment and yellow pigment were found in house excavations and probably served as the 'paint.' The cylindrical 'seals' would have created a long design stripe as they were rolled across the body.

plate 43

It is difficult to reconstruct the types of clothing worn by the people of Chalcatzingo. Although Early Formative figurines from Tlatilco and similar sites show simple skirts and other garments, by the Middle Formative period the figurines wear only headdresses, and explicit body details are lacking. This might imply that the figurines had actually been dressed in tiny cloth garments, but it more likely means that the head and headdress were the only significant portions of the artifact; the body could be neuter and generalized.

Some clothing is shown on people depicted in carvings. These individuals are either elite or observing special ritual roles in some scenes – or both – and their garments may be neither typical of the village nor of everyday clothing. In these carvings the main article of both male and female clothing is a skirt-like garment held in place by a sash wrapped round the waist. The knotted area of the sash is decorated and the sash is longer on males. Some of these skirts are kneelength, others taper sharply from back to front.

In some of the scenes classifiable as depicting more ritual events (Monuments 1, 2), the figures (males) wear short capes. Males seem to wear large headdresses, while the one female depicted in a carving (Monument 21) wears a long, decorated burnouse.

No textile fragments were recovered, and only by analogy to conquest-period indigenous clothing can one understand the materials used for weaving. Textiles from plant fibers other than cotton were probably common, but possibly found mainly among the non-elite villagers. Several fine bone needles suggest some garments made of a fine fiber such as cotton or rabbit fur, while heavy deer-bone awls imply leatherworking.

During the Formative period in Mesoamerica there are no artifacts clearly identifiable as related to the spinning of fiber for cloth. A not-infrequent artifact at Chalcatzingo, and at sites from later periods, is the small ceramic disk made by grinding pottery sherds into small (2–5 cm diameter) circles. These ground sherd disks are frequently perforated near their centers, and are occasionally hypothesized by well-meaning archaeologists to have been used as spindle weights for the spinning of various fibers. However, three types of such disks were actually made: plain, partially perforated, and perforated. While it is possible that the perforated disks were slipped onto a spindle as a fly-wheel-type weight (as were spindle whorls, many hundreds of years later), the plain and semi-perforated disks certainly did not serve such a function. Furthermore, the perforated disks show no wear marks on the central hole, and many of the holes are off-center, a fact which would create an inappropriate wobbling spin. These disks were far more probably tally markers of some type, perhaps functioning in a game such as *patolli*.[63]

plate 44

A final category of artifacts relates to blood sacrifice. Although the child burial at the corner of Chalcatzingo's tabletop altar suggests that some type of human sacrifice played a role in the ritual beliefs at the Cantera phase village, it was probably a minor part, never approaching that of the Aztecs and their contemporaries. Sacrifice at Chalcatzingo seems to have been personal blood sacrifice: drawing your own blood. Such auto-sacrifice was common later both in central Mexico and among the Maya. Some Maya art depicts blood being drawn from the ears, tongue, or penis, and caught on paper to be used ritually.

plate 45
plate 46

Chalcatzingo's blood-letters took two forms, one natural and one manufactured. The few stingray spines found were obviously imports. Thin, finely crafted, long obsidian needles were far more common discoveries. Other objects such as thorns may also have been utilized, but none were located during the excavations.

Although the variety of artifacts excavated permits us to form some basic notion of items important in the daily life at Chalcatzingo, they also present a heavily materialistic view of life. The majority of the artifacts provide few clues relevant to understanding the belief system or religion of the people. Archaeologists at most central Mexican sites can usually progress no further along those lines, but at Chalcatzingo a large corpus of carved art supplies a wealth of data which provide insights beyond the level of non-perishable artifacts. The iconography of some of these monuments is discussed in the following chapter, giving us a rare insight into a set of beliefs which one group was attempting to communicate visually to another.

8 Mythico-religious monuments

The rich corpus of Chalcatzingo's monumental art occurs on two separate and distinct areas of the site. The upper terraces – the public-elite sector of the village, with its platform-mound structures – is the location of carvings which can be related to a theme of rulership (see chapter 5). These monuments are usually portrait carvings, confirming the legitimacy of power of certain individuals.

Monuments bearing themes associated with agricultural fertility or involving masked or non-natural humans or animals are found on the mountain slopes above the settlement itself. One such group of reliefs is executed on natural outcrops high on the mountainside, a second group is carved on large boulders on the talus slopes above Terrace 1. A few other monuments are situated near or within the ancient village area. The dichotomy of themes and locations is not strict, for some portraits are depicted in those more supernatural themes, for reasons that I will discuss below.

The rulership and supernatural themes in the monumental art are also typical of Gulf coast Olmec carvings. That should not be surprising, for the inspirational roots of Chalcatzingo's bas-reliefs came to the highlands from the Gulf coast. Only in the heartland was there a sophisticated stone-carving tradition. None existed elsewhere. At Chalcatzingo, and at the few other sites further south which exhibit Olmec-style carvings, the technology and the iconography arrived fully developed. There were no local antecedents. This was not an idea simply copied from the Olmec centers, but must have involved Gulf-coast-trained artists skilled in stone carving, knowledgeable in the intricate messages conveyed by the iconographic motifs, and bringing with them an artistic sophistication which allowed them to manipulate and adapt the art to a variety of circumstances.

There are some important differences between Gulf coast monumental art and that of frontier sites, and if heartland-trained artists were responsible for the frontier monuments, then the implication is that they were executing a specific sub-style taught them at their Gulf coast centers but not practiced there. In some instances, such as the carvings of personages holding scepter-like objects, the frontier monuments seem to reflect a political-rulership theme, possibly in some manner creating an alliance between the ruler of the frontier settlement and the Gulf coast Olmec. At Chalcatzingo, where there is a greater quantity of frontier art for analysis, it can be seen that heartland religious beliefs were also communicated, and in some instances readapted to the new highland environment.[64]

Heartland Olmec art conveyed a series of ideas, beliefs, and concepts which was already familiar to the peoples living at or around the Gulf coast centers. Because the religion and political situation was understood and familiar, many ideas could be implied and rendered abstractly in the art. An analogy can be made with Christian religious art which carries as its main symbol the cross. Within that shape there is implied a great deal of information which is known and understood by Christians, but which is not at all apparent to anyone unfamiliar with Christian beliefs. The symbolism must be explained to them, its meaning often being taught by the use of accompanying illustrations.

Much of the art of Chalcatzingo served exactly that purpose of explaining the belief system. This art made explicit whatever was implicit in Gulf coast art, communicating those concepts to people who were familiar neither with the iconography, nor possibly with the total range of beliefs.

fig. 5

Monument 1, high on the western face of the Cerro Chalcatzingo, is the largest and most important of six carvings in that locale. A few meters further east Guzmán was shown two others carved on the exposed bedrock.[65] Since these initial discoveries, three other small carvings have come to light nearby, two of which were uncovered in 1972 when our project removed soil from an area of bedrock separating the two carvings seen by Guzmán. All five smaller carvings extend in a line running eastwards from Monument 1.

The symbolism of Monument 1 must be nearly as apparent to the tourist viewing it today as it was to the artists who created it, and, probably, to the villagers of Chalcatzingo who discovered it in 1932. The personage *El Rey* is seated within a highly stylized cave which is not only an earth-monster's mouth but also shaped like mountain glyphs of slightly later date found at the site of Monte Alban in Oaxaca.[66] He is within both the mountain and the earth (the underworld).

Issuing from the cave are large scrolls which seem to represent wind or mist. At the top of the scene are three multilayered trilobed rainclouds from which a fine drizzle (shown by many thin vertical lines) and large raindrops (shaped like large exclamation marks) fall into the cave and across the rest of the scene. Identical raindrop motifs decorate *El Rey*'s tall headdress and skirt-like garment. Also interspersed in the scene are concentric circles, the symbol of the *chalchihuitl* which signified jade and precious water. Several plants are shown growing from the outside edge of the cave-mountain symbol and above the cave.

Readers familiar with the religious beliefs of the Aztecs, as documented by the Spanish chroniclers in the 16th century, and with folk beliefs still held in conservative Indian villages in central Mexico, will see the similarity of Monument 1's scene to beliefs regarding the source of rain. According to these,

Tlaloc, the deity of rain, brews rain in mountain caves and from there distributes it by various means across the countryside. But the concept of caves as entrances to the underworld and thus sources of water and plant fertility was current long before the Aztecs came to dominate central Mexico, as is amply demonstrated by Monument 1.

The principal focus of each of the smaller carvings adjacent to Monument 1 is a small animal facing east, its head tilted to the sky. The animals are in a relatively unweathered state and look like somewhat stylized lizards; similar representations in clay and stone are known from other Formative period highland sites. The tiny creatures are probably saurian sky and earth supernaturals, a concept important on the Gulf coast and apparently widespread throughout Mesoamerica at the time. plate 15

The thematic content of the five small carvings is similar, despite minor variations in the depiction of the animal. Each creature is usually positioned directly over a horizontal S-shaped scroll. Above its head is a rain-cloud motif, a smaller version of those shown on Monument 1. Raindrops fall from each cloud, and on a few of the reliefs an ornate bifurcated scroll emerges from the animal's mouth and extends to the base of the cloud. On the three small reliefs nearest to Monument 1, small squash vines are depicted below the animal and the horizontal scroll.

Because the five small carvings occur one after another on the rock faces east of Monument 1 – *El Rey* – project co-director Jorge Angulo has hypothesized that they were meant to be viewed as a step-by-step visual sequence, beginning with the carving furthest from Monument 1 and working towards it. According to his interpretation, the animals assist in attracting the clouds toward the mountain within which *El Rey* is seated. There the clouds discharge their cargo of precious water, giving sustenance to the plants in the fields below and on the hill itself.[67]

However, even if those carvings were indeed meant to be viewed sequentially, there is no way of knowing which way the sequence was really read. The wind surging from the cave of *El Rey* may be carrying the rain that has been brewed within the mountain cave out of it, eastward (or northward) across the valley, assisted by the animals. In either case it is clear that the association of water and caves (representing the underworld) is of great antiquity in Mesoamerica. The positioning of the carvings around the natural drainage that carries rainwater down the mountainside merely reaffirms their strong association with rain and fertility.

The carvings on the talus slopes above Terrace 1 are very large reliefs. Three were carved on huge boulders, and two on substantial slabs. The four major carvings are spaced about 20 m apart in an east-west line near the top of the talus slope. All the carvings originally faced north. Two of the reliefs on boulders and one of the carved slabs contain enough stylistic similarities and common symbols for them to have been carved at about the same time. They are discussed here in reverse numerical order to aid understanding. They too

29 *Monument 5, a saurian monster and a prone human figure. L. 3.7 m.*

may form a sequence, but because the meaning of these reliefs is not well understood such an idea can only be viewed as a possibility.

fig. 29   The easternmost of the carvings, Monument 5, is on a low boulder which juts from the slope in a way that creates an overhang or niche. The carved area of the rock extends along the boulder's north side and partially into the niche. The scene is of a large serpent-like creature with a crocodilian head. The creature, which faces west, is clearly a mythical composite saurian. It lacks the legs of a crocodile, and has a small fin just behind its head. Its body is covered with V-shaped scales and includes a large X symbol. The tail area is damaged and difficult to reconstruct.

The creature's mouth is dominated by three large pointed upper teeth and a front fang. Projecting forward from the mouth is an unusually long forked tongue. In front of the head and partially covered by it is a human figure as if flung backwards, arms over its head. The human can be interpreted as either emerging from the creature's mouth or being consumed by the fierce saurian.

Although some archaeologists feel that the pointed scales on the creature's body identify it as a 'feathered serpent,'[68] there is really little reason to believe that the 'feathered serpent' so important in the beliefs of many later Mesoamerican civilizations had its roots in the Formative period. The Chalcatzingo saurian is closer to another mythical creature of the conquest-period codices and legends, the *cipactli*, an animal which dwelt in the

30 *Monument 4, two stylized felines pouncing on two prone human figures. 2.5 by 2.5 m.*

primordial sea. Three large scrolls beneath the animal may symbolize such a setting. However, it is highly doubtful that correlations between concepts held during the 16th century and those of the Formative period 2000 years earlier can be demonstrated.

To understand this saurian scene it is probably necessary to comprehend the symbolism on a neighboring relief to its west, Monument 4, executed in the same style. That carving covers a large flat slab of rock which at one time stood erect. Today it lies against a massive boulder on which another relief, Monument 3, is carved. This description follows its original orientation, however.

plate VI

fig. 30

Four figures are displayed in a descending order down the face of the monument. They are alternately a feline, a human, a feline, and a human. Both felines, with their claws unsheathed, appear to be leaping on the prostrate humans who lie with their arms extended above their heads. They are identical in execution to the human grasped in the mouth of Monument 5's saurian creature. This suggests that they are contemporaneous, and are to be considered together as part of a scene, a sequence, or a mythical event. On both monuments the humans are being dominated by animals with supernatural attributes.

The two felines differ markedly from each other. The upper animal is dynamic, implying action and movement. Is mouth is snarling, its gums drawn back exposing its teeth. Its eye is open and the pupil clearly defined. An oval cartouche above the eye, containing an X symbol, indicates that this animal is of the supernatural realm. Small bifurcated motifs decorate the front and top of the cartouche, which may be a variant of the motif that Joralemon has identified as Olmec maize symbols.[69] The feline's ear looks stylized and resembles a later Maya glyph for stars and particularly the planet Venus.

Because both rear legs are extended fully, the lower feline gives a more static appearance. That animal too bears symbols showing it to be supernatural. Unlike its partner, its eye appears as a narrow slit with no definite pupil, although there too the eye is topped by a cartouche with a faint X symbol. A band or stripe begins at the eye and runs down the animal's neck and face, then curves to follow the midsection of the body.

The forehead is decorated with a distinctive plume-like object, while a tall, cleft element, resembling thin 'rabbit ears,' rises from the back of the head; a regular ear is missing. The unusual combination of the plume on the forehead and 'rabbit ears' is repeated on the headdress worn by one of the four humans pictured on Monument 2, another carving of this talus slope group (see later in this chapter).

Perhaps the most interesting feature of the lower feline, and unfortunately one of the least understood, consists of three objects which seem to emanate like sparks from the tip of its tail. Each is tapered in a trapezoidal shape with notched ends, identical to the cleft-jade 'celts' commonly identified in the literature as 'Olmec.' Whether those coming from the feline's tail share the same symbolism is a matter for speculation.

The differences between the two felines, and their positioning in the scene (upper and lower), suggests that they could represent important, interrelated opposites, such as day and night, sky and earth, or life and death. The last interpretation is suggested by the life-like eye of the upper feline and the narrow slit eye of the lower animal.[70] Although several hypotheses have been proposed regarding the meaning of the recumbent human figures, I believe they remain to be adequately explained.

Monument 4 originally stood upright at the eastern side of the large boulder on which Monument 3 is carved. That face of the boulder is deeply pitted, and

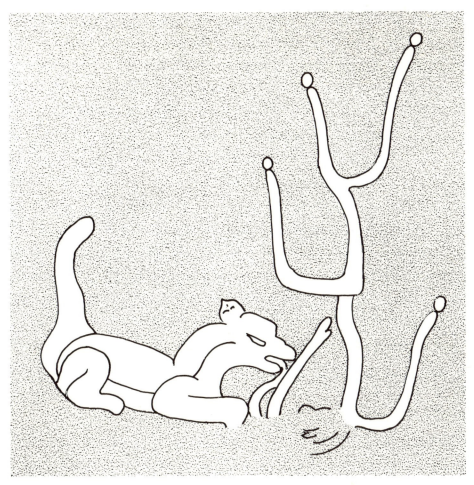

31 Monument 3, recumbent feline licking a large branching object. Left to right 1.2 m.

each of the concavities is striated by hundreds of parallel scratch marks. There is no doubt that those striations are manmade, but why they were made remains elusive. They are not the result of attempts to enlarge the concavities, for the stone-working technology did not utilize techniques which left a multitude of parallel lines. Perhaps these large pits in the rock served ritual functions for either or both monuments, and the striations are the outcome of those rites.

The boulder's vertical north side is carved with a relief composed of two major elements: a large feline and a tall, branching, plant-like design. Unlike the two felines of Monument 4, this animal is at rest. It faces the branching design and its tongue descends to touch one of the lower branches. Or does it? *fig. 31*, plate V In the 1950s fiberglass molds were unfortunately made of several of Chalcatzingo's carvings, including Monument 3. In some instances thin coatings of fiberglass resin were left on the stones after the molds were removed, and just where the tongue appears to touch a branch of the plant-like design, the resin partially obscures finer details of the carving.

Although the felines represented on Monument 4 are supernatural and defy exact identification, the large cat depicted in this relief appears more natural. A line along its midsection indicates it is bi-colored, a trait of the American mountain lion, *Felis concolor* (also known as puma or cougar). The plant-like design is far more difficult to identify. If it is indeed a plant then it may represent one of the several varieties of branching cactus which grow on the hillside nearby, an interpretation I favored at one time.[71]

Somewhat later a visiting anthropologist suggested on seeing Monument 3 that because the branches are each tipped with a small circle – an ancient symbol which could mean water – the various arms of the design might be watercourses. When matched against the pattern of watercourses of the valley north of Chalcatzingo there is some similarity, particularly if the branch touched by the feline's tongue is taken to be the small stream at the base of the site. In such an interpretation the puma would have been a logogram or glyph of the site, and could have symbolized the village (Hill of the Puma?) receiving its liquid sustenance from the stream.

More recently several of us have made close examinations of the carved area around the puma's face and tongue and the adjacent area of the plant-like design. It is clear that some additional complex designs exist there although weathering and the resin deposits confuse the original carved configurations. Details noticed by project co-director Jorge Angulo have convinced him that the object touched by the puma's tongue is an upraised human arm, and that the upper portion of a human figure is emerging from the bottom of the scene.[72] The human's head is partially obscured by the resin. If that is correct, then that relief too depicts a human subordinate to an animal, although there the feline is not aggressive.

The westernmost carving of the talus group, one of the most difficult to see, was among the earliest reported at Chalcatzingo. Sometime after the scene had been carved across the north face of a large boulder, the stone was severely undercut by erosion, causing it to tilt forward until it rested against another rock below it on the hillside. The carved area almost touched the lower rock, and only a narrow crevice existed for access to the carving. However, during Piña Chan's research at Chalcatzingo, portions of the lower boulder were removed with dynamite, exposing the carved scene and rendering it more accessible.

While the three carvings previously described depict humans dominated by animals, this scene is quite different. No animals are represented directly, but the persons are participating in what appears to be a ritual, all wearing masks of the 'bird-serpent' type. As mentioned earlier, on frontier monuments such masks are frequently worn by single individuals who hold a scepter-like object. They occur in other frontier-art contexts as well, including the painting of a

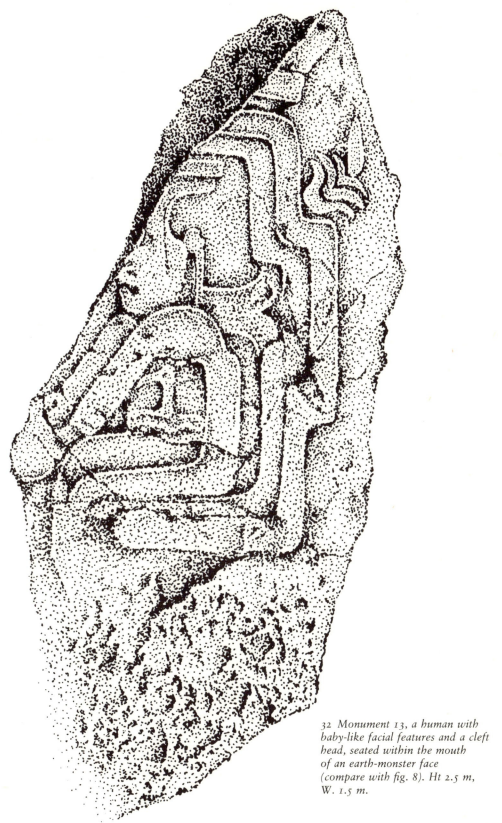

32 Monument 13, a human with
baby-like facial features and a cleft
head, seated within the mouth
of an earth-monster face
(compare with fig. 8). Ht 2.5 m,
W. 1.5 m.

33 A 'Flying Olmec' engraved on a jade object of unknown provenance. A similar engraving was found at La Venta. Both are similar to Chalcatzingo Monument 12. L. 22 cm.

plate 10   human face in profile at Oxtotitlan cave in Guerrero. 'Bird-serpent' masks can be found on only two Gulf coast monuments, La Venta's Stela 2 and Stela 3 (see chapter 9). Since both of those are of the latter part of the Middle Formative period, the 'bird-serpent' mask can be used to date the frontier carvings to the Middle Formative period as well.

    Four persons are depicted on Chalcatzingo's Monument 2. At the right is a seated personage who faces two central figures walking towards him and a third who walks away on the left. The standing figures wear their 'bird-
plates II, 9   serpent' masks so their faces cannot be seen. The seated individual has turned his mask to the back of his head, revealing his face and pointed beard. All the masks seem to cover the entire face instead of simply the mouth area. The seated figure's headdress has a long frontal 'horn' and is reminiscent of one-horned headdresses worn by shamans (medicine men) in some later Mesoamerican art. The only horned headdress currently known in Gulf coast art is depicted on a tabletop altar from San Lorenzo, Monument 14 (see chapter 9), but unfortunately that carving was almost completely erased nearly 3000 years ago by someone who purposely ground away the bas-relief portrait.

    All three standing figures wear short capes, a garment shown in both frontier and heartland art. They also wear waist sashes, and hold out staff-like objects in front of them. The staffs of the two individuals walking toward the seated figure are paddle-shaped and similar in form to agricultural digging sticks used in tropical-forest South America. The object held by the person leaving the scene looks like the stalk of a large plant, or a collection of plumes. Some scholars see the staffs as war clubs, but the carving more probably depicts an agricultural ritual.[73]

    Although the carving does not seem clearly related to its neighbors, their proximity, and the motifs used, indicate that the reliefs are indeed interrelated in some manner. Each individual in Monument 2 has a headdress with

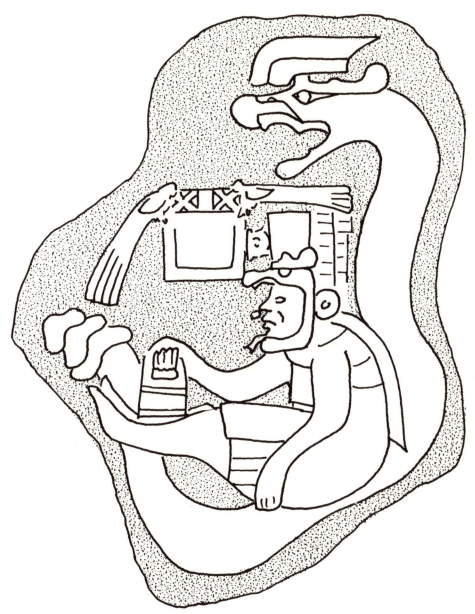

34 *La Venta Monument 19, a person wearing a serpent-face headpiece, seated on the body of a stylized serpent. Ht 95 cm.*

distinctive designs. That of the person standing directly in front of the seated man has the special plume and 'rabbit ears' found on Monument 4's lower feline, and the motifs undoubtedly symbolize the same concept.

Monument 13 is also found on the talus slope, but is downhill from the four large reliefs just discussed, and appears unrelated to them; its closest iconographic similarities are to Monument 1 (*El Rey*) and to Monument 9, the earth-monster face found atop the earthen platform mound. Monument 13 is

fig. 32

the incomplete broken section of another earth-monster face, although its treatment is slightly different from Monuments 1 and 9.

While the earth-monster's large cruciform mouth is nearly identical to Monument 9's, it is not hollow. Instead, carved within the mouth is a seated person facing left. This figure differs from *El Rey* in two respects. Firstly, *El Rey* faces right and is probably a portrait carving; secondly, this seated figure, whose arms extend down towards the feet in a manner typical of Middle Formative Olmec statues, has supernatural attributes including a baby-like face with a dropping mouth and a cleft head, traits also common in Gulf coast monumental art and jades.

Monument 13 is the only carving on the talus slopes and mountainside to have been intentionally broken, a fact which further aligns it with the carvings on the site's terraces, many of which suffered deliberate damage. Thus by looking at locations and themes a mutilation pattern becomes evident. Hillside monuments with their mythico-religious themes such as rain and fertility are untouched, while the political monuments of the public-elite were desecrated.

One of Chalcatzingo's most interesting monuments is Monument 12, a carving with very close stylistic ties to Gulf coast art, found on the site's western periphery, at some distance from the other bas-relief carvings. It is unique in showing a helmeted human shown literally flying through space. His body is extended in a nearly horizontal position, but with one leg slightly bent. His right arm is held forward and bears a torch-like object. His left hand is held to the chest, but the object it grasps has been obliterated by the weathering of the rock surface.

His helmet is the head of an animal, probably an opossum, and his face appears in the animal's mouth. He wears only a short tapered skirt held by a side waistband and long sash. Beneath him is a parrot also in flight, while above him are two long-tailed birds which have no central Mexican prototypes and may represent the tropical quetzal birds of southern Mesoamerica.

The theme of a 'flying Olmec' has several close parallels in Gulf coast art. A flying person carrying a torch in an extended hand is engraved on a small jade object recovered during the excavations at La Venta, and on a second jade object of unknown provenance. Several Olmec art works in a variety of mediums depict persons (but not flying) holding a torch and some form of handstone.[74] A small decapitated carving of this type (Monument 20) was found during our excavations, incorporated into a house foundation.

The person's pose and dress are also similar to the background figures carved in Stelae 2 and 3 from La Venta, and to the seated person depicted in that center's Monument 19. The latter carving shows the individual's head encased in a serpent helmet, the face framed by the open mouth. In form and artistic treatment the helmet is nearly identical to that of Chalcatzingo's 'flying Olmec.' Furthermore, two long-tailed birds appear in front of the serpent mask, making it difficult to believe that the person who executed the

plate 6
plates III, 14

fig. 33

plate 20

figs 40-1
fig. 34

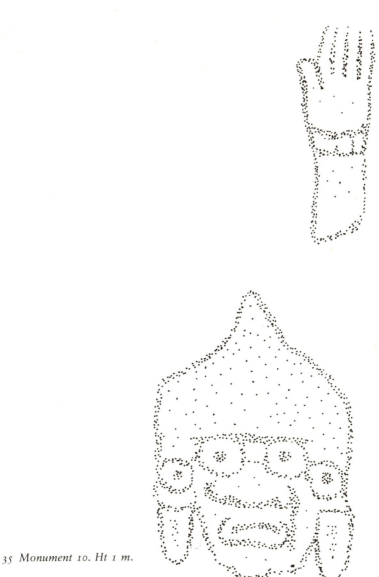

35 *Monument 10. Ht 1 m.*

Chalcatzingo carving was not closely familiar with the La Venta monument and its symbolism, as well as heartland art in general.

The 'paired quetzal-bird' motif may identify an individual important to both La Venta and Chalcatzingo, and in archaeological terms indicates that through this unique, shared motif the two monuments are closely contemporaneous. If the motif is indeed a personal identifier it is of even further interest, for it appears once more at Chalcatzingo, at the rear of the tall headdress worn by *El Rey* (Monument 1).

All three monuments bearing the 'paired quetzal' motif may relate to a type of art which is neither completely political nor entirely mythico-religious, but

121

rather a blend of both. In these examples the identified personage appears in a supernatural setting. In beliefs held by some later prehispanic cultures, deceased forebears became revered ancestors with the ability to mediate with supernatural forces, particularly those responsible for water, rain, and fertility. It is thus possible that some portrait monuments contained supernatural symbolism that confirmed the powers to which the individual portrayed had access.

Although *El Rey* is perhaps Chalcatzingo's best-known example of a revered ruler or ancestor shown associated with supernatural forces, Monument 10 may have had similar connotations, although these are not graphically depicted. It consists simply of a human face and a detached left arm above it, both carved in low relief on the north face of a large boulder at *fig. 35, plate 13* the very summit of the Cerro Chalcatzingo, 300 m above the terraced hillside. To the ancient Mesoamericans, mountain peaks and rain had close associations. As noted in chapter 6, this particular carved human head can be identified by his peaked headdress and unusual facial features as Person D depicted in C8 portrait figurines, and was probably a chiefly ancestor, a mediator with the supernatural forces.

At Chalcatzingo and on the Gulf coast the personification of rulers in monuments and figurines indicates that the ruler had become the focal point of society and the symbol of its well-being. It is probable that in the 'cult of the ruler,' control of supernatural forces was no longer carried out by village shamans, but had passed to the person of the ruler. That does not mean that the ruler was conceived of as divine or the source of those powers, but that he was an intermediary with the ability to manipulate them successfully.

9 Gulf coast Olmec centers

In central Mexico the Middle Formative culture was typified by farming communities which lacked monumental art and any identifiable mounds that might be classifiable as public architecture. However, both these traits are present at Chalcatzingo. They seem essentially restricted to the site and its subordinate villages in the Amatzinac valley, a fact which sets these settlements apart from their highland neighbors.[75]

This special group of traits seems to have derived mainly from the Gulf coast Olmec heartland, perhaps brought to Chalcatzingo by actual Gulf coast elite. And because a few elite may have resided (and died) at Chalcatzingo, the site can be seen, from the point of view of those elite and of the heartland centers, as a frontier outpost. A set of primarily (although not exclusively) elite and ritual traits of heartland origin, intermixed with the generally non-elite highland cultural assemblage, resulted in the special blend of two cultural traditions seen in the archaeology of Chalcatzingo. This is of major importance in terms of the archaeology of the Gulf coast centers.

La Venta, one of the main Gulf coast Olmec centers, is situated on a low, artificially leveled hill, above the floodplains of the Tonala River. The site's significance was first recognized by Frans Blom and Oliver LaFarge during their 1925 journey of exploration along the Gulf coast. Then, in 1942 and 1943, Matthew Stirling conducted excavations there, assisted in his research by Philip Drucker. In 1955 Drucker returned to La Venta accompanied by archaeologists Robert Heizer and Rober Squier to carry out further investigations.[76] All those projects focused on a major plaza-and-mound group which Stirling had christened Complex A.

The plaza is partially delineated by a pair of long earthen platform mounds *fig. 36* which are separated by a space of 39.6 m, the plaza's width. Each mound is approximately 87 m long, with a 16 m-wide upper surface. Their original height was about 2.4 m. A decapitated statue, La Venta Monument 23, was discovered atop the western platform, as were several limestone slabs. Other long platform mounds occur to the south of Complex A, and all are clearly reminiscent of Chalcatzingo's earthen platform, whose upper area also incorporated at least one monument, a number of worked stone blocks, and some elite burials.

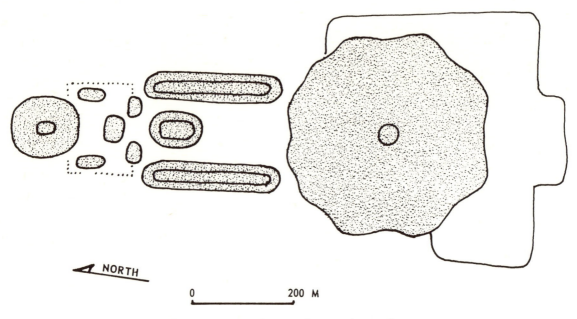

NORTH

0   200 M

36 Map of La Venta's Complex A and pyramid (Complex C).

The archaeologists who worked at La Venta concentrated most of their excavation of Complex A along an imaginary center line bisecting the plaza.[77] On that line, between the platform mounds and near the plaza's midpoint, is structure A–3. That oval mound, slightly over 30 m long, was excavated during Stirling's early investigations at the site. Within the mound and on the center line, those excavations disclosed a large rectangular crypt of sandstone slabs, 11 standing upright to form the sides, and 5 more as covering stones. This crypt is far larger than those at Chalcatzingo, measuring 5.2 m in length by 1.8 m in width, with sides over 1.3 m high. An additional 9 sandstone slabs make up the crypt floor; Chalcatzingo's, on the other hand, lacked floorstones. Thirty-seven jade celts had been placed around the inner edge of the crypt, while the central area was stained with red pigment. Jade beads and two earspools lay within the stained soil as if they had originally ornamented a human interment, but no trace of bone remained.

Also within the mound, but near its south edge, was another red-stained area, again with earspools and beads, arranged as if they had adorned the burial of a child. Four serpentine figurines were found just south of that grave. Several jade and stone artifacts had also been placed along the center line between the two graves.

As Stirling's center-line excavations were extended past the south end of mound A–3, they encountered a pavement of serpentine blocks which had *fig. 37* been laid out in the form of a large mosaic face, nearly 4.8 m by 4.4 m. This was one of three such mosaics found by excavations in Complex A. While frequently referred to by archaeologists as 'jaguar masks,' their correct

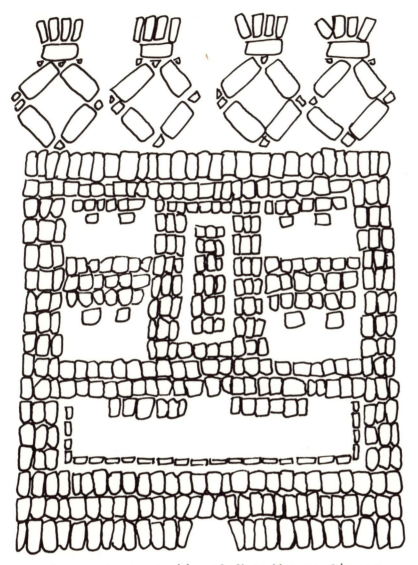

37 *Large mosaic supernatural face at La Venta. Measures 4.8 by 4.4 m.*

viewing orientation ('which end is up?') and their symbolism are still being debated.[78] The generalized term 'supernatural representation' best fits them for the time being.

At the north end of the plaza, and bisected by the center line, is the Ceremonial Court, an open area delineated and surrounded by low rectangular platforms and a major mound. This smaller plaza is important not only for its buried offerings, but also because it had been completely enclosed by a fence of vertical columns of basalt. Naturally occurring columnar basalt is known from a number of locations around the world, including one area of the

Tuxtla mountains, northwest of La Venta. The basalt columns, each weighing about one ton, were also incorporated into other constructions in the Ceremonial Court area.

Mound A–2, at the extreme north of the Ceremonial Court and Complex A, yielded three tombs to the excavators, each still along the center line. The largest and most spectacular was Tomb A, a rectangular structure with its 1.7 m-tall side walls formed by 3 m-long columnar-basalt pillars deeply embedded side by side into the earth. The tomb structure measured 4.4 m long and 3.7 m wide. Its north side, apparently the tomb-opening, was formed by five leaning columns. Additional columns formed the roof.

The tomb's floor was paved with limestone blocks and covered with a coating of clay. Red-pigment stains, together with fragments of human bone and jade artifacts, disclosed the location of what had been two burials, both at the tomb's south end. Associated with the 'burials' were four greenstone and jade figurines: a seated woman with a tiny iron-ore mirror pectoral, and three babyface humans in the same style as the figurine recovered at Chalcatzingo from a crypt grave (see chapter 6). A tiny pair of hands carved in jade, a jade replica of a stingray spine, several actual spines, and a shark's tooth were also found.

South of this magnificent columnar-basalt tomb, and still within the mound's interior, lay eleven smaller pillars of basalt, placed side by side in an east-west direction. A few feet beneath those the excavators revealed another area stained with red pigment and a great number of jade artifacts. Those included thirty-five celts, earspools, quantities of beads, and a concave mirror of polished iron ore. No bone fragments were found by the archaeologists, so it is possible that this was a special cache of jade rather than a human interment.

fig. 38 A few meters further south the excavation trench laid bare a large sandstone sarcophagus, 2.8 m long, 0.96 m wide, and about 0.85 m tall. A slightly larger sandstone slab served as its cover. When opened, the sarcophagus was found to have been intentionally filled with clay. When that was removed, jade earspools, a jade figurine, and a jade 'awl' were revealed, but again there was no hint that this large sandstone box had held a human burial.

The exterior of the sarcophagus is of great interest, for its surface had been carved in bas-relief, giving a face and limbs to the box so that it represented a saurian supernatural. I stress the saurian aspects – the serrated eyebrows, long slit-like eyes with turned down ends, and short stubby legs – for, in the early history of Olmec studies, creatures with these attributes were called 'jaguars,' and Olmec iconography became wrongly associated with jaguar supernaturals. Scholars are now recognizing that crocodile-like supernaturals and not jaguars pervade Olmec art. The saurian in its varied forms seems to have been associated with fertility, life, water, etc. The jaguar had far less importance, perhaps serving as a mediator with the supernatural realm and, as such, a patron of shamans and rulers. Both saurian and jaguar continued in those general roles in the religion of the Maya almost a millennium later.

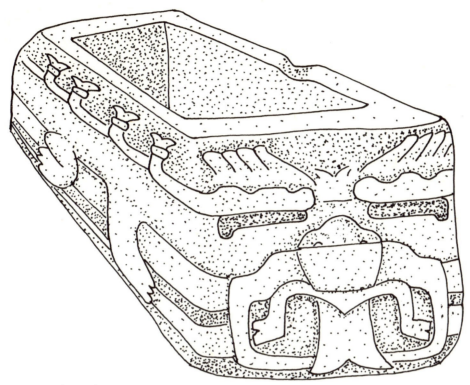

38 Sarcophagus from La Venta, Mound A-2. L. 2.8 m.

Even more spectacular finds awaited the archaeologists. Excavations in a small platform mound within the Ceremonial Court, about 12 m southeast of Mound A–2, uncovered a magnificent cache of sixteen greenstone figurines and six celts. This cache is unique, for the objects had been erected to form a small scene. Eleven of the smoothly polished jade and serpentine figurines,   plate 73 each about 17.5 cm tall, had been placed upright in a semicircle facing towards the celts, which had been erected vertically as if representing stelae. Four other equally high-quality figurines were placed in a line, as if walking toward the center of the semicircle. The sixteenth figurine is the focus of the group's attention. He is different, having been manufactured from a grainy granitic stone, and he stands with his back to the row of celts (stelae) facing the others in the group. With this cache we are perhaps gaining a look at a recreated ancient Olmec ritual, something we could never reconstruct from the normal type of data unearthed in an excavation.

Not all the discoveries in the Complex A area can be discussed here, but another group of equally spectacular discoveries deserve mention. These were offerings not of quality, the equivalent of jade figurines, concave iron-ore mirrors, or carved sarcophagi, but offerings of unbelievable quantity and thus, overwhelming human labor – massive burials of tons of serpentine slabs, placed as layered 'floors' in great pits excavated deep into the Ceremonial Court. Typical of these is the offering buried beneath the platform mound at the southwest corner of the Court. The pit holding the offering covered an area of over 280 sq. m and had been dug to a depth of 7.3 m. Into that huge excavation 1000 tons of serpentine blocks had been piled in 28 courses, each layer of blocks separated by a smaller one of bluish clay. A large mosaic mask had been laid above this and then covered with olive clay. A thick mottled pink clay separated the offering from the platform above it.

Three such massive offerings are now known. Two are on the center line: one beneath mound A–2 with its basalt-pillar tomb and sandstone sarcophagus, the second beneath the Ceremonial Court. A third lies under the Court's southwest platform. If the center-line symmetry holds true, another massive offering should lie below the northwest platform and the mosaic mask uncovered there in 1943. The mosaic mask on the center line at the south edge of mound A–3 could also mark a massive offering, but it was not disclosed in test excavations.

These massive offerings present a formidable problem of interpretation. Unlike the highly visible monumental edifices, here labor was invested in burying objects of worth far from sight. That each may have consumed as much as 1000 tons of serpentine blocks is astonishing when it is remembered that La Venta is situated on a river floodplain, far from any stone sources.

The stone for the colossal heads, stelae, altars, the columnar basalt, the serpentine blocks, luxury greenstone, and even stone for common grinding tools, all had to be brought to La Venta from elsewhere. Basalt for monuments generally came from the Tuxtla mountains to the north, presumably on rafts following rivers and the coast. The acquisition of the serpentine blocks used in the massive offerings, while perhaps not as bulky or heavy, required a different and more arduous effort, for the nearest serpentine sources occur in the mountains of the Pacific coast, at least 100 miles distant as the crow flies, but further as human carriers walked.[79]

If one person could have carried 100 lbs of serpentine per trip, 20,000 loads would have been required to amass the serpentine for the southwest platform offering alone. Each huge burial of serpentine required a no-less massive investment of human labor, for the ancient Mesoamericans had no beasts of burden to assist them. That labor came from a relatively small labor pool; there is no evidence for large population densities at, or near, the Gulf coast centers.

The south end of the Complex A plaza at La Venta is dominated by the site's great pyramid, named by the archaeologists Complex C. This tall mound, which sits atop a low, wide platform, rises 32 m above the plaza, the mounds of Complex A, and the Ceremonial Court. Its original shape has also become the subject of controversy in recent years. After the 1955 transit survey of the mound's surface, Drucker, Heizer, and Squier reconstructed the earthen pyramid as originally having been rectangular with sloping sides. More recent topographic mapping under the direction of Heizer led him to the conclusion that the mound had actually been circular, with fluted sides. That, he suggested, may have been an attempt to replicate a cindercone volcano such as found in the Tuxtla mountains, mountains perhaps sacred to the Olmecs.[80]

There are arguments in favor of each viewpoint. In 1897 an engineer measuring the altitude of the San Martín Pajápan cindercone volcano found an Olmec statue at its highest point, indicating that the volcano had been special to the Olmec. This lends clear support to Heizer's hypothesis. The people of the Gulf coast would not have been alone in the world in replicating the sacred mountains of their cosmologies as pyramids – it was a fairly common occurrence in antiquity.

plate 68

A strong argument against the round-fluted-pyramid theory is simply that the structure has never been adequately investigated. Torrential rains have subjected it to their erosive powers for over 2500 years. We should be surprised if its surface were *not* somewhat fluted!

Furthermore, it may be incorrect to consider that this tall mound was Mesoamerica's first pyramid structure, as is believed by some scholars. Recent investigations in the state of Chiapas, southwest of the Gulf coast, have discovered large Middle Formative period ceremonial centers which are architecturally as complex as La Venta. They include major pyramid-like mounds, as well as long platform mounds. What those sites lack are the stone carvings and buried offerings of the Gulf coast.[81] Until further work is carried out though, we will not know which came first.

La Venta has the distinction of having more known monumental carvings than any other Olmec center. Unfortunately, not all the carvings were found by archaeological research. Many were unearthed during recent construction activity, for the area is becoming quickly engulfed by an oil refinery and its associated boom town.

Four colossal stone heads, the most famous of Olmec monuments, are known from the site. Three stand over 2 m tall, and all four weigh between 12 and 24 tons each. Each is the head of a personage wearing a helmet-like headpiece. The front of the helmet covers the forehead to just above the eyes, while sidestraps frame the face, which is well modeled and heavy featured. The eyes are normally heavily lidded, the nose is broad and flaring, while the lips are frequently thick and everted.[82] The first was found in 1862 at Tres Zapotes and described as 'Negroid.' While descriptive of the general facial features, this identification has been taken too literally by some authors, for such characteristics are common among Indian groups on the Gulf coast and elsewhere in Mesoamerica, and are not indicative of transatlantic contacts.

plates XV, 77

The colossal heads are most certainly portrait monuments of specific individuals, and probably represent the various rulers who had governed the centers. Although at first glance these massive heads resemble each other, distinctive physical characteristics, such as prominent teeth, clearly differentiate them. The design found in each helmet is likewise distinctive and was apparently an identifying 'glyph' for the individual portrayed, supplementing the physical characteristics.

Equally impressive in size and skilled workmanship are La Venta's massive tabletop altars, some of which may have been the prototypes for Chalcatzingo's Monument 22. The largest and most spectacular is Altar 4, a monolith as tall as a man – 1.6 m – and which is 3.2 m long and 1.9 m wide. The major feature of the altar, like most others, is the niche carved in its front face. Within the niche is a seated personage in high relief, the ruler to which this altar was dedicated. He leans slightly forward with arms extended to grasp thick coiled ropes running along the altar's base to the side carvings. His identifying headdress is damaged, but careful inspection shows it to be the head of a bird with the beak broken off, most probably a harpy eagle. The niche interior is covered with feathers, as if this ruler wore a feathered cloak.

plate VIII

Depicted on the sides in bas-relief are seated figures, although that on the altar's right side has been nearly completely ground away. Both individuals had been connected to the ruler on the altar front by the thick rope. Although they have been identified as 'captives,' they far more probably represent relatives, bound to the ruler by the rope of kinship, an ancient Mesoamerican concept.[83]

Directly above the niche and the ruler, on the altar's projecting ledge, is a stylized jaguar's face. The body or pelt of the jaguar is carved along the top of the altar, the remainder of the ledge being decorated with a motif identifying it as representing the earth. The total symbolism of the earth, with the niche leading beneath the earth, can be tied to two major themes: the power of the supernatural realm, and divine birth. The supernatural-power aspects of the iconography have been mentioned in chapter 5: to be seated at the entrance to the underworld displays access to the powers governing rain, crop fertility, and other important forces.

Several highly mutilated Gulf coast monuments have been interpreted as depicting a sexual act between a human and a jaguar. Such a mythical union, taking place in the underworld, may have been conceived of as resulting in the origin of the Olmec people. Other data suggest it also served to create dwarf-like creatures with rainmaking powers. On some altars, such as La Venta's No. 5, the niche is occupied by a human holding a dwarf-life baby with supernatural characteristics. Carved in bas-relief on the altar's sides are other humans carrying babies. The theme of human holding a supernatural dwarf-like baby is also found on Gulf coast statues. However, since the jaguar–human copulation monuments are decapitated and battered – a treatment usually accorded only to portrait monuments – the union may have been between ruler and jaguar, mythically creating the next generation of rulers and legitimizing their right to rule.[84]

plate 74

plate 75
plate 72

Embellished with their rich iconography, the massive altars apparently served a semi-functional purpose, that of the chiefly throne. The jaguar pelt carved atop Altar 4, and repeated with variations on other altars, is analogous

39 Polychrome mural above the cave entrance at Oxtotitlan cave in Guerrero. A human seated on the altar-like supernatural's face. W. c. 3.8 m, Ht 2.5 m.

and perhaps even antecedent to the jaguar thrones of Maya rulers. That altars were indeed thrones is suggested by one of the rare Olmec period paintings to survive the ravages of time. That painting, in the state of Guerrero, Mexico, far from the Olmec heartland, is executed on the cliff face above one of the two mouths of Oxtotitlan cave. The positioning of the painting above the actual cave is surely not coincidental, and visually demonstrates the equation of caves with altar niches. The polychrome painting includes the face of a supernatural *fig. 39* creature similar to that decorating Chalcatzingo's tabletop altar. Seated over the supernatural's face, one leg casually dangling across its front as if it were an altar face, is a richly attired personage. His easy pose suggests that the monstrous face serving as his seat is an inert object, such as an altar, rather than an active supernatural creature. In the cavern below this mural is a painting showing a human male mating with a jaguar.[85]

If my hypothesis is correct (that colossal stone heads and personages seated within niches are portrait carvings of Olmec rulers identifiable by headdress motifs) and if we are right in thinking that rulers had multiple monuments erected – then we should begin searching for and finding repetitions of these identifying motifs among the carved art. The hunt for comparisons is complicated by the fact that most Olmec monumental art was severely mutilated, frequently by decapitation of statues whose heads have very rarely been recovered archaeologically. Chalcatzingo's Monument 17, found in an elite burial, was therefore a rare and fortunate discovery (see chapter 6). In analyzing Gulf coast portrait carvings I have managed already to make one pairing, although surprisingly it involves not only two different types of monument, but two different centers as well.

The helmet of La Venta's Colossal Head 4 bears a bird's foot with talons, what I have called the 'eagle-foot identifier.'[86] The personage's face is distinctive because he is shown with 'buck teeth,' and in most monumental art teeth are not shown. Among the carvings from the site of San Lorenzo now displayed at the museum in Jalapa, Veracruz, is Monument 14, a tabletop altar whose front face is badly damaged by both mutilation and erosion. Its theme is the same as La Venta's Altar 4 discussed above, a ruler seated in the frontal niche and holding ropes which run to the persons carved in bas-relief on the altar's sides. The person once shown to the ruler's right has been almost completely removed by deliberate grinding. The bas-relief to the ruler's left shows a seated individual wearing a hat-like headpiece which is decorated with a large eagle's foot. This personage is also depicted as having prominent front teeth, and there is little doubt that it is the same individual as portrayed in the La Venta colossal head. If I am correct in identifying the rope running between the San Lorenzo ruler (shown in the front niche) and the person on the

40 Stela 2, La Venta. Standing figure with elaborate headdress surrounded by smaller persons wearing 'bird-serpent' masks. Ht 3.1 m.

side (a La Venta ruler as demonstrated by the colossal head at that site), then this monument communicates a kinship tie between the rulers of these two important Olmec centers. Such kinship may have been actual or mythical.

The kinship theme between monuments implies that an important form of alliance existed between La Venta and San Lorenzo at one period in their history (c. 950 BC). If the rope between the men is, however, interpreted as 'capture,' a theme particularly common in Late Classic period Maya art, the implication would then be of warfare between the major centers and cultural but not political unity across the Gulf coast.

Archaeologists and art historians generally place the Olmec colossal heads and monolithic altars in the Early Formative period, or pre-900 BC. Olmec statuary seems to cover the whole span of the culture, a time range of c. 1100 to 500 BC, but stelae and large stone slabs with bas-relief carvings may date late in the Middle Formative period, perhaps 750–500 BC.

fig. 40 The two major La Venta stelae, both from the Middle Formative period, are portrait monuments. Stela 2 depicts a standing ruler in frontal view, wearing an extremely tall and complex headdress, whose design includes both the ruler's identification motif and an additional motif which seems to be the glyph of an important ancestor. The motif matches that of Colossal Head 1, identifying that Early Formative ruler as the ancestor. Either a genealogical continuity in rulership took place at La Venta over a period of four or five centuries, or the ruler shown in Stela 2 fictionalized his descent from an important earlier ruler to strengthen his legitimacy to rulership. Six small masked figures appear in the background of the scene.[87]

fig. 41 Stela 3 is somewhat different, for it depicts two personages facing each other. Again small human figures 'float' in the background in poses reminiscent of Chalcatzingo's 'flying Olmec' carving. Both major figures wear elaborate headdresses. The person on the right has sharp facial features which include an aquiline nose and a beard (possibly false). Most of his body is missing for a large area of the relief has flaked away. A fragment of relief behind him suggests he stood in front of an entrance to the underworld. While the figure to his left is in relatively good condition, the face is missing, apparently intentionally destroyed. Remaining fragments of the facial area suggest it was wide and heavy in its features, like portraits of Gulf coast rulers.[88] Although fanciful interpretations have been offered for this scene, it most probably commemorates a meeting between two persons of chiefly rank, with the La Venta ruler represented on the left.

For many years the research at La Venta provided the only good archaeological data available for Olmec culture. But although Drucker, Heizer, and Squier were able to develop a sequence of four major building

41 Stela 3, La Venta. Two standing personages and smaller background figures, at least one of which wears a 'bird-serpent' mask. Ht 4.3 m.

periods for Complex A and the Ceremonial Court, none of the excavations provided a long stratigraphic record of cultural development at the site. The monuments, the elaborate architecture, and the various offerings, large and small, seemed to have 'appeared suddenly' with no antecedents.

Because La Venta could not document Olmec origins, some scholars began to look outside the Gulf coast for cultural ancestors. Furthermore, the La Venta research had not found residential structures and La Venta became thought of as a 'vacant center' with only a small resident population composed of the ruler, priests, and caretakers. This view quickly became applied to other Olmec heartland centers as well.[89]

As the reader can see, these assumptions, whether ultimately proved to be valid or invalid, rest on extremely incomplete data. La Venta's excavations had been almost exclusively restricted to the Complex A-Ceremonial Court area, a small public-ceremonial area of the site which certainly should neither be viewed as representative of La Venta nor as reflecting the totality of Olmec culture. No intensive survey of the site or of the surrounding area was made to locate residences. Other architectural complexes remained untouched, including a separate public-ceremonial area called the Stirling Group, an area with a different directional alignment to its structures and with several important Early Formative style monuments. Today, because of a Pemex oil refinery being constructed on the site, any more research there may be virtually impossible.

Some of the data on Olmec culture lacking at La Venta have been supplied by recent archaeological excavations at San Lorenzo, 51 miles southwest of La Venta and about 30 miles south of the Tuxtla mountains. This large center is located on a hilltop plateau overlooking the Chiquito and the Coatzacoalcos rivers. Two smaller Olmec settlements, Potrero Nuevo and Tenochtitlan, lie near the base of the hill. All three sites were seen by Stirling in 1945, and some excavations were carried out in 1946. However, it is the research project of Michael Coe in the late 1960s that illuminated San Lorenzo and brought about a more detailed understanding of Olmec culture in general.[90]

Most of the architecture visible on the San Lorenzo plateau is contemporaneous to Middle Formative La Venta, or even to more recent prehispanic periods. Earlier structures were destroyed or buried by these later rebuildings. The site's architectural pattern resembles that of La Venta, with plazas formed by long earthen platform mounds, and a major central 'pyramid.' But excavations show the zenith of San Lorenzo to have been prior to 900 BC, in the Early Formative period. This is also demonstrated by its many Early Formative style monuments, including colossal heads and tabletop altars, and by the lack of large stelae.

If excavating in La Venta's Complex A did little to elucidate Olmec cultural development, and left the impression that Olmec culture 'appeared suddenly,' the San Lorenzo project provided a far better stratigraphic record which also had much greater antiquity. The earliest materials recovered at the site date to

plate 76

fig. 42

plates 79–80

Human figurines

47 Babyface figurine head with noticeable teeth. Amate phase. Ht 4 cm.

48 Early Formative period 'pretty lady' (type D1) figurines. Amate phase. Ht of central head *c.* 4.5 cm.

49 Type C9, or so-called 'babyface' figurine heads. Amate phase. Ht of head on left *c.* 3 cm.

Babyface figurines

69 Greenstone babyface figurine similar to those found at La Venta, but of alleged highland central Mexico provenance.

70 Clay figurine with baby-like facial features. Found at La Venta.

71 Hollow babyface figurine, found during road-construction work at Atlihuayan, Morelos, in central Mexico. The figure wears the skin of a supernatural saurian creature.

72 Polished stone statue of a human holding a dwarf-like baby with supernatural features.

73 Cache of polished stone babyface figurines and celts forming a ritual scene. This is our only evidence for rites actually performed. From La Venta.

Colossal heads

77 La Venta Colossal Head 1. Ht 2.4 m.

78 Colossal stone head found at Tres Zapotes in the early 1860s.

79 San Lorenzo Colossal Head 1, during excavation.

80 San Lorenzo Colossal Head 2. The author believes the bird (probably parrot) symbols in the headdress are the identifying glyph of the Olmec ruler portrayed in this head.

81 The rear of San Lorenzo Monument 52, cut as a drain stone.

82 A heavily mutilated statue, Monument 23, La Venta. Compare with Chalcatzingo's Monument 16 in plate 19.

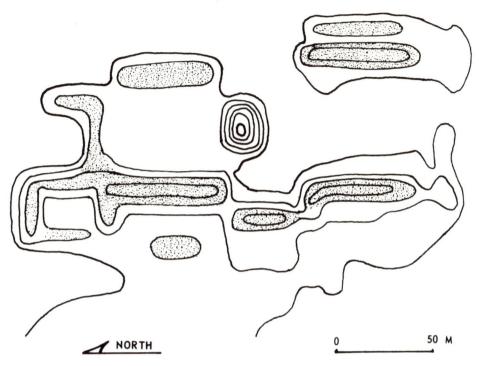

NORTH

0   50 M

42 *Map of the North, Central, and South Courts at San Lorenzo. Shaded mounds are presumed to be Middle Formative period.*

about 1500 BC. At that time the San Lorenzo hilltop seems to have been the location of two hamlet-sized farming settlements, with nothing grandiose about them. The ceramic vessels employed there were patterned after far more elaborate pottery from the same period on the Pacific coast of southern Mexico and Guatemala. That is the period Michael Coe calls the Ojochi phase, and he likens the culture at San Lorenzo to a 'country cousin' of Pacific coast developments.[91]

The archaeological investigations disclosed the increasingly complex lifestyles of the hilltop occupants in about 1350 BC. That is the Bajio phase, a period in which the traits leading to fully-fledged Olmec began appearing. Although the evolutionary trend is best seen in the San Lorenzo data, it took place throughout the Gulf coast.

In Bajio phase San Lorenzo, a massive public-works project began, and the natural hilltop was gradually transformed into a huge artificial plateau. The task was accomplished by adding great quantities of earth and gravel to create an enormous plateau. The soil was brought in baskets from elsewhere on the hill or from the flatlands, and required the marshaling of a vast human laborforce. The terracing at Chalcatzingo is a minor feat in comparison, but since, as with Chalcatzingo, we have no good idea how long the plateau-building took, it is difficult to estimate the yearly labor necessary. The end result is amazing, however, for the plateau they built is 1200 m long and over

500 m wide, and the earth and gravel fill extends in places to a depth of 7 m.

The society's perceived need to build this large plateau, and the planning and labor organization required to erect it, demonstrate that Bajio phase culture had undergone an important transformation. The 'country cousin' had come of age and now outshone Pacific coast relatives. Unfortunately the 'whys' for the huge construction effort and its original function – if different from its later use as ceremonial architecture – remain obscure. Only a few of Coe's excavations reached down to Bajio phase deposits, and the only architecture exposed was a portion of a simple red-sand platform about 2 m tall.[92]

During the Bajio phase some ceramic styles began developing in the direction of the major types found during the Olmec period at San Lorenzo. Those include differentially fired white-and-black wares, and hollow pudgy figurines (unfortunately lacking their heads). The latter may have been the precursors to the hollow babyface figurines found a few hundred years later, and usually thought of as one of the hallmarks of Olmec culture.

Exactly when San Lorenzo and other parts of the Gulf coast became Olmec is a subjective decision. The so-called identifying traits – such as monumental architecture, carved monuments, differentially fired ceramics, pottery with 'Olmec' motifs, babyface figurines, and the use of jade – appear individually over a long period of time, not together and suddenly. In the Chicharras phase, which began about 1250 BC, there is some archaeological evidence for stone monuments, hollow clay babyface figurines, and greenstone jewelry. Jade artifacts were not common until after 900 BC.

With the coming of the San Lorenzo phase in 1150 BC, the culture at San Lorenzo can certainly be called 'Olmec,' although that 'Olmecness' was part of a gradual evolution. Colossal heads and tabletop altars were being made (and mutilated). Ceramic vessels bearing incised decorative-symbolic motifs are common, and were used by Coe as a major diagnostic to separate the Chicharras and San Lorenzo phases. In addition to the many mound structures which presumably covered the plateau, Coe's work uncovered evidence of another construction feature apparently common at heartland centers: a series of shallow 'lagoon' areas, connected to an intricate group of U-shaped stones set end to end and capped by stone slabs to form a long drainage system. Such systems have been found at La Venta and San Lorenzo, and the presence of drain stones at Laguna de los Cerros and Tres Zapotes indicates the presence of similar constructions there too. At San Lorenzo, Coe's excavations discovered a drain system in which the first U-shaped stone was beautifully carved on its outer surfaces in the form of a werejaguar baby figure (San Lorenzo Monument 52). San Lorenzo Monument 9, reported by Stirling, is a large basin carved in the form of a duck, but with a rectangular notch on one side the exact shape to accept a drain stone. This duck basin was apparently at the edge of the plateau and functioned as the end piece of a drainage system, the water from the drain pouring into the large cavity in the duck's back.[93]

plates XII, 81

The functioning of the lagoon areas and their drainage systems can only be conjectured. The fact that monumental carvings depicting natural and supernatural creatures are incorporated into the drainage systems indicates they had religious and ritual importance. But for the Olmec they also represented significant engineering achievements, not only for the complexity of the stone drain system, but for the construction of the lagoons as well. As mentioned earlier, the San Lorenzo plateau is an artificial construction built up over several hundred years. Much of the fill material is gravel, hardly the type of substrata in which to build lagoons meant to hold water. The solution arrived at by the inhabitants of ancient San Lorenzo was identical to that used by geologists today in the western United States to build lakes and ponds in areas of porous soils. Examination of the San Lorenzo lagoons showed them to have been lined with bentonite clay which rendered them impermeable. The same procedure is still valid nearly three millennia later.

Coe's San Lorenzo excavations, when coupled with other research on the Gulf coast, indicate that the finds there were not part of something which 'appeared suddenly,' nor for which origins must be sought elsewhere. The archaeological record bears witness to an indigenous evolution of the culture today called Olmec. The heartland was its birthplace.[94]

The old hypothesis that the Olmec originated outside the Gulf coast rested not only on the lack of clear antecedents to La Venta's Complex A artifacts, but equally on the mistaken belief that tropical environments prohibited rather than nurtured cultural growth. Early models of agricultural development were drawn from Sumeria, Egypt, and the Basin of Mexico. Scholars from temperate climates failed to see how anyone, ancient or modern, could live comfortably in hot, humid, tropical environments or could be sufficiently productive using simple but extensive slash-and-burn agricultural methods in the tropical forests. Subjectivity overshadowed scholarship. The San Lorenzo excavations by Michael Coe began when a newer generation of scientists was rethinking the productivity of tropical ecosystems.

Coe's research was indeed not restricted to excavations, but included an analysis of present-day ecology and land-use in his research area. That important work showed that the levees flanking the rivers below San Lorenzo had rich agricultural potential, perhaps surpassing other areas, such as the Basin of Mexico, prior to the development of intensive irrigation systems. By planting on the river levees and the hillsides below the site, the people of San Lorenzo would have had substantial food supplies, and an agricultural surplus which they could use to support a small number of non-farming artisans and other specialists, and which they could trade for exotic goods such as jade.[95]

Due to the everpresent constraints of time and budget which plague most archaeological research, the San Lorenzo project gave priority to excavating certain ceremonial areas, and to obtaining an excellent stratigraphic record. Although a small number of residential mounds was found, few were excavated. Thus it is still uncertain whether major Gulf coast centers were truly 'vacant' or whether they were genuinely 'occupied.' For many decades archaeologists considered the great centers of Mayan civilization in the jungles of southern Mesoamerica to have been 'vacant.' Then, in the 1960s, excavations and settlement surveys at the site of Tikal, Guatemala, proved exactly the opposite case – Tikal had been a near-urban metropolis.[96] The same is apparently true of most other major Mayan centers. Since the Olmec 'vacant'-center model was originally borrowed from Mayan archaeology, it rests on very shaky foundations.

No attempt has been made here to describe San Lorenzo's rich corpus of monuments. Many were found by Stirling, but an even greater number appeared during Coe's excavations. In fact Coe added a new twist by using a magnetometer to locate buried stone monuments. The technique was perfect for San Lorenzo – an area with no native stone – but it would not work well at Chalcatzingo. In locating previously unknown carvings Coe also discovered an interesting phenomenon. In two instances the buried carvings occurred in groups, including some monuments set one after another in a line. Almost all the carvings he uncovered had been mutilated, some by decapitation, others by effacement through grinding, statues by breaking off body parts, and in the case of some altars, by knocking off huge pieces. The destruction is an awesome accomplishment for a culture whose largest tools (as recovered archaeologically) seem to have been hafted stone axes. Because of the number of mutilated monuments, Coe has hypothesized that San Lorenzo and other Gulf coast centers suffered a revolt which he believes swept the heartland in about 900 BC, a revolt during which monuments were destroyed.[97] However, an alternative interpretation of the causes of monument mutilation is made in the next chapter, using data from Chalcatzingo.

It is difficult to compare La Venta and San Lorenzo as Olmec centers since the best-known and excavated areas at each are not contemporaneous. Both were occupied during the Early Formative period, for they have monuments typical of that time (colossal heads, tabletop altars). The data from Coe's excavations at San Lorenzo show that it lacked Middle Formative period stelae, indicating that it had declined greatly in importance by 700 BC. It was at about the same time that La Venta reached its great importance, with numerous carvings, significant mound architecture, and the elaborate offerings of the Complex A–Ceremonial Court area.

By 700 BC Chalcatzingo had its own long platform mound, Olmec-style frontier art including stone stelae portraying rulers, monument mutilation in the heartland pattern, elite burials within stone-slab crypts, and several other traits that demonstrate a significant relationship and interaction between that highland center and one or more Olmec centers on the Gulf coast. In the next chapter I discuss my hypotheses on why Chalcatzingo may have been one of the few Middle Formative period centers with such a significant link to the Gulf coast Olmec. I also use Chalcatzingo's archaeological data to illuminate further the nature of Gulf coast Olmec society.

10 Chalcatzingo and the Olmec

Although valuable archaeological data were recovered from the excavations at La Venta and San Lorenzo, they illuminate primarily ceremonial and elite aspects of Olmec life. So most current reconstructions of Olmec culture and its development remain very much in the nature of hypotheses based solely on hypotheses, rather than on substantial archaeological evidence. It is also doubtful that archaeological knowledge of the Gulf coast will improve significantly in the future unless steps are taken immediately to save the region's major archaeological sites. The Gulf coast has fallen victim to 20th-century progress. La Venta has been nearly completely destroyed by a petroleum refinery, while oil drilling, land clearing, ploughing for major agricultural developments, and expanding populations threaten other sites throughout the Gulf coast. Site destruction is an irreversible action.

In view of the nature of Gulf coast archaeology and its current problems it is gratifying that the research at Chalcatzingo recovered data that could be used to illuminate certain aspects of heartland Olmec culture. The data are variable: in some instances they merely point out certain artifact types which have not received proper recognition in the heartland and should be investigated further. One example is the three-prong cooking-brazier that is common in Chalcatzingo households but has not been reported at other central Mexican sites. Although a utilitarian rather than an elite artifact, we suspected that it may have been one of the 'intrusive' traits of Gulf coast origin. An examination of archaeological collections from Gulf coast Olmec centers discovered them there too. Virtually nothing about houses or cooking practices is currently known in the heartland, but it seems probable that cooking-braziers were used at least by elite members of the society there.

In other instances the data from Chalcatzingo have shed new light on important aspects of the heartland belief system. The numerous C8 portrait figurines, typical of Chalcatzingo but rare elsewhere in the highlands, stimulated us to recheck the Gulf coast data for similar artifacts. The published figurine data from the heartland are small, but portrait figurines do seem to be present in Middle Formative assemblages, and I believe those at Chalcatzingo to be Gulf coast inspired. The presence of chiefly portraits in both monuments and figurines implies a cult of the ruler transplanted into

Chalcatzingo and most easily recognizable there, but one highly significant in the heartland. The Chalcatzingo research has awakened us to the extreme importance placed on the ruler by Gulf coast society.

At one time it was fashionable to search for Olmec origins everywhere but in the heartland, and frontier art was often hypothesized to be ancestral to that of the Gulf coast. Chalcatzingo did not escape claims that it was a center of origin, but one hopes that such guesses have been put to rest by both the San Lorenzo data and those from Chalcatzingo.[98] It seems possible now to conclude that the artists who executed the first bas-reliefs at the site were from the Gulf coast, and were most probably trained at La Venta. As mentioned earlier, the Chalcatzingo reliefs are the first evidence of carved-stone art in central Mexico. There was no local carving tradition; the technology and iconography arrived fully developed.

Chalcatzingo's carvings are Gulf coast Olmec in general style, but differ in the way they communicate their ideas. This distinct approach we have called the frontier art style, one which could only have been executed by persons with an intimate understanding of the heartland style, for it openly symbolizes concepts which are abstracted in Gulf coast monuments. This means the audience for which the art was intended was unfamiliar with the underlying symbolism in Olmec art, and for whom it was simplified. Chalcatzingo's art was thus not intended for the ruler or highest-ranking members of the society, a few of whom may have come from the heartland at one time and have had some familiarity with the iconography of monumental art; it was for highlanders – other than the chiefs – from villages elsewhere in the Amatzinac valley, or from other parts of central Mexico. Those were people who interacted in some manner with Chalcatzingo, and who would be influenced by the power which the monuments showed Chalcatzingo and its ruler to possess.

Fifty years ago, when archaeologist Eulalia Guzmán first visited Chalcatzingo, she was shown a decapitated seated statue.[99] Such sculptures, presumably ruler's portraits, have since been found at both San Lorenzo and La Venta; Chalcatzingo's is similar but somewhat blockier in its execution. Over the decades, however, no one questioned why that seated figure, so similar to heartland statues yet found such a great distance from the Gulf coast, should also have been mutilated. Its decapitation is particularly puzzling since central Mexican societies at that time totally lacked a tradition of monuments, let alone of their mutilation. Is the published explanation for heartland monument mutilation, which ties the breakage to acts of iconoclasm or revolution, applicable to a monument at a far-distant 'frontier' site?

Guzmán's headless statue is not the only Chalcatzingo monument which suffered destruction. I have previously mentioned several damaged carvings uncovered during our research, including a decapitated head found in an elite crypt grave, and mutilated stelae. However, the hillside reliefs with their mythico-religious themes were untouched. Mutilation can therefore be seen as directed towards the site's 'political' monuments. Such a pattern of destruction is generally true on the Gulf coast as well.

If it is difficult to attribute the mutilation of Chalcatzingo's stelae and statuary to a group of iconoclasts and a revolution sweeping through the Gulf coast centers, it is equally hard to explain heartland mutilation in that manner. An inspection of the evidence underlying the accepted hypothesis of Gulf coast iconoclasm and revolution shows it to be merely the fact that monuments were broken – no more, no less. But, in fact, that same evidence indicates that the destruction of monuments was not a one-time act. It was, rather, something which apparently took place regularly. With a few exceptions, every portrait monument in the heartland was mutilated. This means that monuments personifying each and every ruler over a long time-span were destroyed. Obviously it can be hypothesized that every one of those portrait monuments was standing exposed at 900 BC and thus vulnerable to destruction when the alleged revolt took place. But what of the mutilated Middle Formative period monuments carved after 900 BC? A similar revolution would have had to occur then, with exactly the same pattern of breakage by iconoclasts. That is highly unlikely!

The revolt hypothesis neither accounts for the damage to Chalcatzingo's monuments, nor explains why a decapitated statue head would have been placed with an elite burial. This last burial provides an interesting start to understanding mutilation. In analyzing every Gulf coast monument together with Chalcatzingo's, it can be seen that destruction is focused primarily at the head and face of portrait monuments.

While a statue can be broken at the neck area and the head taken away to be placed with a burial or elsewhere, on thick stelae in which the portrait is executed in bas-relief, it is far more difficult to fracture the stone so that just the head is removed. Chalcatzingo's Monument 27 was broken into three sections. The base remained in place, while the piece bearing the portrait face (but not the entire head) was carried away. Monument 28, on the same terrace, was apparently far too thick to break effectively at the head area, so the facial area was instead simply ground away, a technique also employed on La Venta's Stela 3. All these types of mutilation are common in the heartland.

plate 82

The removal of faces from monuments by grinding illuminates one of the rules underlying mutilation. The people in the heartland and at Chalcatzingo had the ability to break large monuments if they so desired. However, breakage of such carvings is difficult to control and to confine to a specific area. It appears that they felt the monument must break correctly, for a poor break would have been worse than none at all. In that case defacement by grinding seems to have been preferred. Further, a massive carving could have been indiscriminately broken into many pieces and the facial and head chunks removed, but this also seems to have been unthinkable in most cases. Such haphazard breakage was consciously avoided, indicating clearly that mutilation was for some other purpose than mere destruction.

The portrait head with the elite crypt burial suggests that a particular statue had been decapitated immediately following the death of the individual interred in the crypt grave. This leads to a hypothesis regarding the cause of mutilation which seems to fit more closely the data on hand: mutilation of monuments took place at the time of death of the person portrayed.

There could be many explanations for why a person's monuments were destroyed at that time. The mutilation may, for example, have 'protected' the living members of the society from any supernatural powers they believed remained encapsulated in the carvings. Or breakage might have released a deceased ruler's soul from his monuments.

This ritual hypothesis better explains why the earliest known monuments, the latest Olmec monuments, and monuments at Chalcatzingo, far from the heartland, were mutilated. The practice in fact did not end with the Olmecs, for similarly damaged carvings continue into the period of Maya civilization in southern Mesoamerica, possibly for the same reasons. Furthermore, because data from both San Lorenzo and La Venta indicate that many monuments were buried in discrete groups, it is probable that each group relates to a specific deceased ruler. Thus each group has the potential, when properly analyzed, for providing significant data pertaining to individual rulers, their genealogical ties, and their important symbolic motifs.

Although it is evident that Chalcatzingo's association with the Gulf coast made it different from other highland settlements, just what that association was has perplexed scholars since the site's rock carvings were first recognized as Olmec-like. Explanatory hypotheses such as wandering Olmec missionaries, military conquest by heartland armies, and mass migrations from the heartland are neither logical nor fit the most recent archaeological data. Those data indicate that Chalcatzingo's settlement had more than religious contacts with the heartland, that the contacts give every evidence of having been peaceful, and that probably only a very small number of people at the site were actually from the heartland or descended from heartland peoples. The village was not an Olmec colony. The vast majority of the site's artifacts show that in basic cultural details it was central Mexican and non-Olmec.

The stratigraphic evidence shows that many of the heartland traits in ceramics showed up gradually over a period of several hundred years, and not rapidly as a colonization would imply. It is unfortunate that no reliable method exists for dating the carvings, to ascertain when they appeared and to see whether they too represent a gradual development. They show enough stylistic difference to indicate that they are not all exactly contemporaneous, but they still may only span all or part of the 200 years of the Cantera phase, when Chalcatzingo and its heartland influences were at their peak.

Chalcatzingo was not established as a highland colony by peoples from the Gulf coast. Its importance seems to have preceded its close heartland connections, and its early history set the stage for the major role it was to assume later.

While in comparison to neighboring areas the valley of the Amatzinac River is agriculturally marginal, within the valley itself Chalcatzingo's location is the best available in terms of total resources. The hillslope soils are rich and productive. The small spring at the base of the hill provided drinking water. While maize-farming was surely practiced, the prehistoric Mexican diet was always supplemented by hunting and the collecting of wild plants and fruits. Accessibility of such wild resources was always therefore an important consideration in selecting a location for settlement, and here Chalcatzingo was in a favorable position. The site is located at the junction of the valley's two major vegetation zones. To the north lay the forested woodlands of the central valley, with a variety of tree crops, medicinal herbs, and deer. In contrast, the plains to the south were arid, dominated by thorn acacia and cacti, a habitat for rabbits. The mountainside and river *barranca* created other distinctive ecological zones worth exploiting.

In addition, the Amatzinac valley is relatively rich in natural geological resources. The hills skirting the southwest flank contain iron ores in both powdered and natural metallic form. Analyses of the ore pieces found in the workshop area of Terrace 1 show that they were brought to Chalcatzingo from sources in those hills that were of such significance that the first Spanish iron smelter in Mexico was built only a few miles north of Chalcatzingo and used ore from those mines.[100]

Also to the south of Chalcatzingo was an important deposit of kaolin clay, mined during the *hacienda* period to give a white color to sugar made from local sugar-cane crops. At Chalcatzingo, kaolin presumably from that deposit was used to create the surface color of Middle Formative white pottery, and to whitewash the clay exteriors of houses.[101] But kaolin is not a common clay, and, during the Middle Formative period, white-slipped ceramics are abundant in many areas of Mesoamerica. If kaolin was the primary clay used for the slip, then many villages had to import kaolin for use in pottery manufacturing or to acquire the already-manufactured vessels through trade.

Chalcatzingo supported the largest Amate phase population in the entire valley. By size alone it had local importance. But its central location gave added status, for its people could serve as intermediaries for the goods from one area of the valley which made their way to other local villages. Initially such exchanges probably relied on a network of personal relationships, but this redistributive role for the village gained importance with time. Forest products from the high altitudes of the Popocatepetl volcano at the north end of the valley may well have been exchanged for the southern valley's powdered iron ore, to be used for body painting. Kaolin may have passed in every direction through the network.

The redistributive role for the village soon encompassed materials from beyond the valley's borders. Obsidian, the volcanic glass which was the favored cutting tool of ancient Mesoamerica, came to the Amatzinac valley from sources to the northeast of the Basin of Mexico. Greenstone from the mountains of Guerrero, shell from distant oceans, and pottery typical of areas to the southeast, all moved into Chalcatzingo and out again to local settlements. Villages with the role of local redistribution were to be found within each geographical area of the highlands, interacting both locally, and inter-regionally with each other.

While the mountainous highlands are rich in geological resources, the tropical floodplains of the Gulf coast are not. Yet in the rapidly evolving cultural complexity of the heartland, the rulers and elite came increasingly to depend on a variety of objects, made of imported raw materials, to communicate their status and power. The stone for monuments was brought from the Tuxtla mountains, serpentine blocks from the Pacific coast, greenstone, jade, iron ore, mirrors, and other status exotics arrived by long-distance acquisition networks. Even obsidian and stone for maize-processing tools were imported.

During the Early Formative period, prior to 900 BC, the material from outside the heartland was apparently acquired indirectly through a series of established networks. Although some scholars have hypothesized that Gulf coast peoples made direct contacts with far-distant source areas during that period, recent archaeological data do not support such a theory. We cannot speak of Olmec frontier sites at this time.

However, during the Early Formative period the Gulf coast was not the only area of Mesoamerica increasing in complexity. Although only the Gulf coast visually communicated parts of its belief system in non-perishable stone art, many areas saw the rise of important centers. The elite at these other centers, like the Gulf coast elite, desired to communicate their power through similar exotic objects, and the demand for exotics increased rapidly. The great distance separating greenstone sources, as an example, from the Gulf coast, and the informal nature of the exchange network by which goods ultimately reached the heartland, was such that as the demand increased along the network route, the desired materials were siphoned off by other centers before reaching the Gulf coast. The supply of status goods to the Olmec centers was no longer assured. It is probably that situation, rather than revolt, which was partially responsible for San Lorenzo's decreasing importance during the period after 900 BC.

The ultimate response from the heartland to the problem was the initiation of a different means of acquiring the desired goods. In order to bypass the siphoning effect caused by an informal acquisition network, significantly more direct contacts took place after 900 BC with distant redistribution centers that had access to important materials. This can be thought of as a formalization of the network of supply. Chalcatzingo became one of the few and special supply nodes. The manner in which the relationship between supplier and heartland recipient was arranged is perhaps documented through the female personage depicted in Monument 21: an alliance stabilized by the marriage of an elite Gulf coast woman with the ruler of Chalcatzingo.

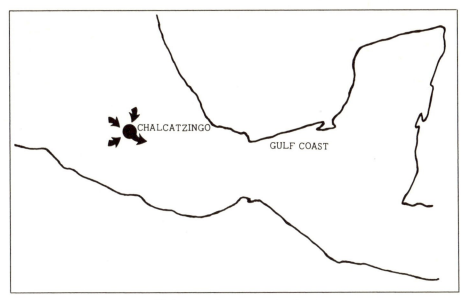

43 *Chalcatzingo's gateway-city function.*

But of the many highland sites which served important roles as redistributors of regional raw materials, why was Chalcatzingo chosen? The answer seems to lie again in its geographical location. Chalcatzingo is situated at the southeast edge of a closely knit cultural sphere which had existed in the Basin of Mexico-Morelos area since about 1300 BC. As a redistribution center located beside a cultural boundary it could serve not only its own region, but also centers across the boundary to the east. That interaction is documented by the site's archaeological record.

Secondly, but relatedly, is the point that the topography of the central Mexican mountain masses and valleys makes the natural communication route between the central highland sphere and the rapidly evolving societies of southern Puebla, Oaxaca, and the Gulf coast, pass via the southeast boundary. Chalcatzingo, with its already-established eastward contacts, was thus situated at the geographic and cultural gateway between a large area of highland central Mexico and the route to the Olmec heartland.

By 700 BC Chalcatzingo can be described as having functioned as a 'Gateway City.' The term is used by geographers for settlements in frontier regions through which resources from an extensive hinterland are funneled toward a major center or centers.[102] In the case of Chalcatzingo, resources from areas such as the Basin of Mexico (obsidian for example), from western Mexico (iron ore, greenstone), and from Morelos (kaolin, iron ore), could be collected for transportation toward the Gulf coast and possibly other southern areas. The elite of Chalcatzingo presumably directed the acquisition and dispersal of the various materials.

fig. 43

The sites of Chalchuapa, Abaj Takalik, and several others along the Pacific coastal mountain slopes in Guatemala and southern Mexico, contain frontier Olmec style carvings, though in far lesser numbers than Chalcatzingo.[103] These too were apparently linked to the Gulf coast through alliances commemorated in art, and these centers fulfilled functions similar to Chalcatzingo's. Their resources probably included cacao beans from the tropical piedmont slopes, obsidian from sources in highland Guatemala, and high-quality nephrite jade from Guatemala's Motagua valley, all of which moved along a Pacific coastal route before crossing the isthmus to the Gulf coast. There is a possibility that the Gulf coast centers controlled much of the commerce in these goods and served as middlemen in their distribution to other areas of Mesoamerica.

The Olmec achievement was based on two major factors: a productive food base, and their long-distance acquisition network for a variety of 'status' goods. That this development took place on the Gulf coast rather than in some other area is probably explained by the availability on the Gulf coast of highly fertile river-levee lands whose rich crop-yields could supplement the simpler slash-and-burn rainfall-dependent farming of the low hills which dot the coastal plain. At 1000 BC this productivity would have far surpassed that of the Mexican highlands, until the innovation of intensive irrigation agriculture. The agricultural system of the Olmec heartland apparently created crop surpluses which allowed the Olmec chiefs to import into their centers goods not obtainable locally. Those imports included massive blocks of stone from which to carve monuments glorifying the ruler and visually depicting his links to the supernatural realm, and exotic items such as jade, again for the use of the chiefly ruler and probably also for those few elite people tied to him through descent from a common 'royal' ancestor. In the beginning such imports may have only been for local consumption, but by 900 BC they had become an important factor in the heartland economy and gradually a new role was assumed, that of distributor, with commodity control carried out through alliances with settlements far distant from the heartland, such as Chalcatzingo.

The ruler of a Gulf coast center was clearly a powerful individual. He was portrayed in both stone and in ceramic figurines, but he was probably not a 'god-king.' One reason for his power is visually displayed on some of his monuments, for he is shown at the entrance to the underworld, demonstrating that he (and probably also his ancestors, the previous rulers) controls the many supernatural powers affecting the lives and agriculture of the Olmec people. Contrary to some scholarly opinion, the Olmec do not seem to have conceived of, or to have worshiped, a group of formal deities. Instead the ruler, through his access to natural forces, mediated with those forces and controlled them. The supernatural creatures depicted in a variety of Olmec art forms represent aspects of those forces (rain, water, etc.) and not specific 'Olmec deities.'

There is no real evidence for warfare between heartland centers, and the political situation may have been one primarily of cooperation rather than competition. Monument mutilation was not the result of revolt or of hostilities, but seems to have taken place soon after a ruler's death, with the intent perhaps of protecting the society from the supernatural powers embodied in the monuments but left uncontrolled at the ruler's death. When a new ruler took control of a center he erected his own monuments which showed his control and his right to rule.

The demise of Olmec culture probably took place gradually and may have been due in large part to a technological innovation which slowly spread through Mexico's upland valleys: intensive irrigation agriculture. This new farming system made possible a crop productivity far greater than that of the Gulf coast, and was applicable to much larger expanses of fertile land. Supported by this new productivity the highland populations increased rapidly and so did their demand and competition for 'status' goods such as jade and cacao. New and larger highland centers arose and the focus of cultural growth shifted there, leaving the Gulf coast far behind. The new centers disrupted and reorganized the economic networks in their favor, leaving little if anything to sustain the material needs of the few Olmec centers, who were ill-equipped to compete for the control of distant resources. As the Gulf coast centers declined in economic importance, and as new economic power centers arose in the highlands, the frontier alliances likewise fell apart. A gateway-city function for Chalcatzingo was no longer possible and its regional importance was usurped by other centers. The settlement was abandoned about 500 BC.

Epilogue

plate X

Following Chalcatzingo's decline the site was only occasionally reoccupied during the next 1500 years. A few figurine heads found on the surface, and several shallow burials with grave offerings, indicate that around 300 BC a few families may have briefly settled on some lower terraces to farm the hillside. However, they built no substantial structures and left almost no remains.

The only major reoccupation of the hillside took place around AD 400, at a time when the large urban city of Teotihuacan in the eastern Basin of Mexico-dominated central Mexico. Three structures from that time are visible today at the site: the round pyramid and a secondary platform both at the northwest corner of Terrace 1, and a ballcourt a few meters to the northeast of those. The pyramid had been built onto the western end of the long Middle Formative earthen platform mound, and portions of the platform mound's north side had been modified to serve as one side of the ballcourt. These Late Classic period public structures had been faced with a coating of lime plaster. Several Late Classic subsurface lime kilns were found which had penetrated and partially destroyed Cantera phase house walls. A few residential structures were also uncovered during our research, but Late Classic Chalcatzingo was a small and minor settlement.

Teotihuacan influence was strongly felt in the Amatzinac valley, as is particularly reflected in the pottery which, although probably locally made, is identical to that from the metropolis. Interestingly, it was the drier southern valley which felt Teotihuacan's impact most strongly. A dramatic population shift to the south took place during that period, a move apparently due to Teotihuacan's desire for one particular commodity, cotton. This is one of the few crops that can be grown well in the southern valley, and although the hypothesis needs to be tested archaeologically, it is probable that the southern area was a major cotton producer and under substantial Teotihuacan control. In fact the southern valley was important only as long as Teotihuacan was dominant in central Mexico. Our settlement-pattern data show that as Teotihuacan's power began to wane, the population of the southern valley likewise slowly diminished. With the collapse of Teotihuacan's power about AD 750, the northern Amatzinac valley regained its numerical dominance, while the arid south returned to cacti and thorn acacia. Chalcatzingo was reoccupied during the period of the gradual northward resettlement.[104]

One of the most surprising aspects of Late Classic Chalcatzingo is the abundance of painted rock art. These depictions consist primarily of crude stick figures painted in red. Many occur in shallow caves in the saddle area separating the Cerro Chalcatzingo and Cerro Delgado, others in caves high on the Cerro Delgado, and several groups have been found on giant boulders at the southwest end of the Cerro Chalcatzingo, far from the site itself. The paintings can be dated because a few of the more elaborate examples contain symbols common in Late Classic central Mexican art.

Evidence of Late Classic occupation at Chalcatzingo is not restricted to the terraced hillside. A stretch of land between the northeastern side of the Cerro Delgado and the river *barranca* became the site of a small ceremonial center which survived until about AD 1350, the Middle Postclassic period. This area, known as Tetla (in *Nahuatl*: 'rocky place'), has several pyramids, large platform mounds, and a ballcourt. A limited excavation there by our project uncovered a four-room house dating to *c.* AD 1200.

Our excavations of caves on the Cerro Delgado yielded artifacts contemporaneous with the Tetla residential structure, including some remarkably well-preserved wooden artifacts and plant remains. These include spun and raw cotton (and one cotton boll), loom fragments, a few tiny remnants of woven textiles, string made from plant fiber, and food remains including maize cobs and seeds. The seeds had been gathered from wild plants native to the mountainside.

Evidence of Postclassic period resettlement of the terraced Formative village area is lacking, yet one public-ceremonial structure was found on the talus slopes immediately below the Monument 2 carving. At the very beginning of the project, when brush was being cleared from the entire hillside, the workers discovered fragments of plaster in the soil and several unnatural rock lines. When time permitted, the hillside was investigated carefully and it quickly became apparent that the slope below Monument 2 had been modified about AD 1200 as a 'shrine' area by the construction of a very broad stone stairway interspersed with platforms and rectangular 'altars.' The entire shrine area had been stuccoed and probably painted as well. Several fragments of large ceremonial braziers were recovered during the excavations. The location of this structure directly at the base of Monument 2 is probably not coincidental. The Middle Postclassic occupants of Tetla apparently revered that carving, whatever it meant to them, and consecrated it by building the shrine and by performing ceremonies. It is even possible that this is the shrine mentioned as existing in the area by Padre Durán (see chapter 2), to which people from throughout the region traveled to make offerings and give prayers.[105]

Visiting Chalcatzingo

The archaeological zone can be visited in an easy one-day automobile excursion from Mexico City or from Cuernavaca, Morelos. Both of these cities are connected by excellent highways with Cuautla, Morelos, the jumping-off point to the site. Visitors should bear in mind that only snack foods and soft drinks are available in the village of Chalcatzingo, so it is advisable to eat somewhere such as Cuautla, or to carry a picnic lunch. Water should also be taken.

fig. 44 From Cuautla the visitor should take Highway 140, east out of the city. Although the highway is not well marked, it is the only paved road running eastward. After 12 miles the traveler arrives at the only major (paved) crossroad along the highway. From this point the twin peaks marking the site can be seen ahead, to the right of the highway. The Cerro Jantetelco dominates the landscape to the north of the road.

To reach Chalcatzingo it is necessary to turn south at the highway junction, towards the town of Jonacatepec. Just over a mile along this road are two signs announcing that the village of Chalcatzingo can be reached by a small road leading eastward. That road is paved only as far as Monte Falco (the former *hacienda* Santa Clara), where it becomes all-weather gravel for the remaining short distance to the village.

For visitors lacking an automobile there is a bus service between Cuautla and Jonacatepec. Taxis can be hired in Jonacatepec for the short trip to Chalcatzingo, and arrangements made with the driver for a return trip later in the day.

A recently constructed cobblestone road leads from the southeast edge of the village to the site, a major improvement over the footpath that existed when our project began. Automobiles can be safely parked at the village plaza, or driven to the foot of the archaeological zone. Whether walking or driving to the site, visitors should ask directions. Some villagers and children occasionally make themselves available as 'guides' for a small fee. The Mexican government maintains guards at the archaeological zone to prevent vandalism. They are knowledgeable, can answer questions, and point out the location of the various monuments.

The *El Rey* carving, Monument 1, and those in its immediate area, are usually best photographed just before noon, when the sun is high but still in the eastern sky. Most other carvings are illuminated by afternoon sunlight.

In addition to the hillside bas-reliefs which have attracted visitors to Chalcatzingo for decades, many monuments recovered by the archaeological research described in this book have been maintained for easy viewing. Those include the tabletop altar and patio, many stelae, the Terrace 6 platform and its in-situ stela, and the Classic period ballcourt and pyramid. Some of those areas have been fenced and roofed to prevent damage. Some of the protective roofs are visible as you approach the site from the village.

A number of artifacts from the excavations, as well as rubbings of some carvings, are on display in the Palacio de Cortez museum in Cuernavaca. The headless statue (Monument 16) first reported by Guzmán, and a reproduction of Monument 2 (made from a fiberglass mould) can be seen in the National Museum of Anthropology in Mexico City. A guidebook in Spanish to the site is also available at both museums.[106]

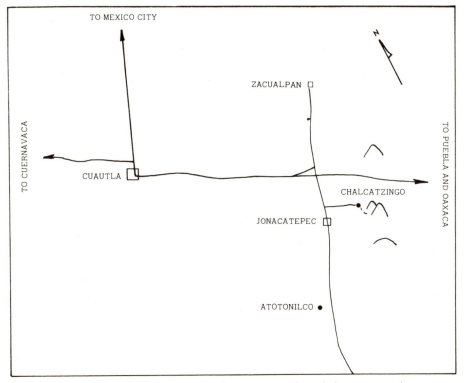

44 *Road map to Chalcatzingo. Distance between Cuautla and the major road junction near Chalcatzingo is 12.5 miles.*

Chronological table

YEARS BC	PERIOD	CHALCATZINGO PHASES	GULF COAST PHASES	
			San Lorenzo	La Venta
500			Palangana	4
600	MIDDLE FORMATIVE	Cantera		
700				3
800			Nacaste	2
900		Barranca		
1000			San Lorenzo	1
1100	EARLY FORMATIVE			
1200			Chicharras	
1300		Amate	Bajio	
1400			Ojochi	
1500				

Notes

Preface

1 National Science Foundation grants GS 31017, BNS 71–03773, and BNS 80–13770.
2 See Grove in press. A summary of the excavation results was also published in Grove et al. 1976.
3 Jorge Angulo, *Chalcatzingo, Morelos, Mexico: Guia de la Zona Arqueologica*, Instituto Nacional de Antropologia e Historia, 1979.

Chapter 1

4 Coe 1968.
5 Matthew W. Stirling, 'Great Stone Faces of the Mexican Jungle,' *National Geographic Magazine* 78 (1940), 309–34; 'La Venta's Green Stone Tigers,' *National Geographic Magazine* 84 (1943), 321–32; Matthew W. Stirling and Marion Stirling, 'Finding Jewels of Jade in a Mexican Swamp,' *National Geographic Magazine* 82 (1942), 635–61.
6 Coe and Diehl 1980.

Chapter 2

7 C. R. Twidale, 'Granitic inselbergs: Domed, block-strewn and castellated,' *Geographic Journal* 147 (1981), 54–71.
8 Fray Diego Durán, *Book of the Gods and Rites and the Ancient Calendar*, University of Oklahoma Press (1971), 257–8. David Grove, 'El Teocuicani: "cantor divino" en Jantetelco,' *Boletin del INAH* 3, Epoca 2 (1971), 35–6.
9 Guzmán 1934, 237–51. Other publications dealing with the carvings include Carmen Cook de Leonard, 'Sculptures and rock carvings at Chalcatzingo, Morelos,' *Contributions of the University of California Archaeological Research Facility* 3 (1967), 57–84; Carlo Gay, *Chalcatzingo*, Akademische Druck-u. Verlaganstalt, Graz, Austria, 1971; and David Grove, 'Chalcatzingo, Morelos, Mexico: a reappraisal of the Olmec rock carvings,' *American Antiquity* 33 (1968), 486–91.
10 Román Piña Chan, *Chalcatzingo, Morelos, Mexico*, Direccion de Monumentos prehispanicos, Informes 4, Instituto Nacional de Antropologia e Historia, Mexico, 1955.
11 David Grove, 'The Pre-Classic Olmec in central Mexico: site distribution and inferences,' *Dumbarton Oaks Conference on the Olmec*, Dumbarton Oaks Research Library and Collection, Washington, DC (1968), 179–85.
12 George Vaillant, *Excavations at Zacatenco*, Anthropological Papers 32, Part 1, American Museum of Natural History, New York, 1931; and *Excavations at El Arbolillo*, Anthropological Papers 35, Part 2, American Museum of Natural History, New York, 1935.
13 See Miguel Covarrubias, 'Tlatilco, Archaic Mexican Art and culture,' *Dyn* 4–5 (1943), 40–6; Román Piña Chan, *Tlatilco*, Serie Investigaciones 1 and 2, Instituto Nacional de Antropologia e Historia, Mexico, 1958; Muriel Porter, *Tlatilco and the Pre-Classic Cultures of the New World*, Viking Fund Publications in Anthropology 19, New York, 1953; Ignacio Bernal 1969, 136, 189.
14 Paul Tolstoy and Louise Paradis, 'Early and Middle Pre-Classic culture in the Basin of Mexico,' *Science* 167 (1970), 344–51.
15 David Grove, *San Pablo, Nexpa, and the Early Formative Archaeology of Morelos, Mexico*, Vanderbilt University Publications in Anthropology 12, Nashville, 1974.
16 See Grove 1974.

Chapter 3

17 See note 10, Piña Chan 1955, 26; and note 9, Gay 1971, 106–7.

18 See note 10, Piña Chan 1955, 7–8.

19 Ibid, map 2.

20 The maps were made by the Compania Mexicana Aerofoto, S.A., with funds provided by a grant from the National Geographic Society.

21 See Kenneth Hirth, *Pre-Columbian Population Development Along the Rio Amatzinac*, PhD Dissertation, University Microfilms, Ann Arbor, Michigan, 1974; 'Teotihuacan regional population administration in eastern Morelos,' *World Archaeology* 9 (1978), 320–33; 'Formative period settlement patterns in the Rio Amatzinac valley,' in Grove in press.

Chapter 4

22 Christine Niederberger, *Zohapilco, Cinco Milenios de Ocupacion Humana en un Sitio Lacustre de la Cuenca de Mexico*, Coleccion Cientifica 30, Instituto Nacional de Antropologia e Historia, Mexico (1976), 256–7; Kent Flannery et al. 1981, 65.

23 See notes 13 and 15.

24 See for example, Keith Dixon, 'Ceramics from two Preclassic periods at Chiapa de Corzo, Chiapas, Mexico,' *Papers of the New World Archaeological Foundation* 5, Orinda, California, 1959; and Flannery 1976, figs 9.2, 9.3.

25 The analysis was conducted by Ann Cyphers Guillen, lab director of the Chalcatzingo project, who is now with the *Instituto de Investigaciones Antropologicos* at the National Autonomous University of Mexico (UNAM) in Mexico City. She is also author of the chapter on Chalcatzingo's ceramics in Grove in press.

26 See R. A. Donkin, *Agricultural Terracing in the Aboriginal New World*, Viking Fund Publications in Anthropology 53, University of Arizona Press, Tucson (1979), 22, 131.

27 See notes 12, 14, 22.

28 Jeffrey Parsons has recently reported at least one site in the southern Basin of Mexico with possible Middle Formative mounds. However, the site had several prehistoric occupation periods and, until excavated, the dating of the mound architecture remains uncertain. See Jeffrey Parsons et al., *Prehispanic Settlement Patterns in the Southern Valley of Mexico*, Memoirs of the Museum of Anthropology 14, University of Michigan, Ann Arbor (1982), 97–105.

Chapter 5

29 Guzmán 1934, figs 12, 13.

30 Kent Flannery and Joyce Marcus, 'Evolution of the public building in Formative Oaxaca,' *Culture Change and Continuity*, Academic Press, New York (1976), 213–15.

31 Stanley Boggs, 'Olmec pictographs in the Las Victorias group, Chalchuapa archaeological zone, El Salvador,' *Notes on Middle American Archaeology and Ethnology* 99, Carnegie Institution of Washington, Washington, DC, 1950; Susanna Ekholm-Miller, *The Olmec Rock Carving at Xoc, Chiapas, Mexico*, Papers of the New World Archaeological Foundation 32, Brigham Young University, Provo, Utah, 1973; David C. Grove and Louise I. Paradis, 'An Olmec stela from San Miguel Amuco, Guerrero,' *American Antiquity* 36 (1971), 95–102.

32 David Grove, 'Olmec monuments: mutilation as a clue to meaning,' in Benson 1981, 49–68.

33 See V. Garth Norman, *Izapa Sculpture*, Papers of the New World Archaeological Foundation 30, Brigham Young University, Provo, Utah, 1976.

34 See Ann Cyphers Guillen, 'The role of a woman in Formative exchange,' in Kenneth Hirth (ed.), *Early Trade in Mesoamerica* (in press), University of New Mexico Press, Albuquerque.

35 See for example David Grove, 'Olmec altars and myths,' *Archaeology* 26 (1973), 128–35; see note 31.

36 The chronology and building sequences were interpreted by William Fash, Jr, in 'The altar and associated features,' a chapter in Grove in press.

Chapter 6

37 Chalcatzingo's houses are described in detail in Mary Tenner and David Grove, 'The settlement and its architecture,' a chapter in Grove in press.

38 The stimulus for this interpretation came from a paper by James Garber, 'Patterns of jade consumption and disposal at the Late Preclassic center of Cerros, in northern Belize,' read at the Dumbarton Oaks Conference on Jade, in December 1980.

39 Jane Pires-Ferreira, 'Shell and iron-ore mirror exchange in Formative Mesoamerica, with comments on other commodities,' in Flannery 1976, 311–26, and *Formative Mesoamerican Exchange Networks with Special Reference to the Valley of Oaxaca*, Memoirs of the Museum of Anthropology 7, University of Michigan, Ann Arbor, 1975.

40 See Marcia Morales, 'Chalcatzingo burials as indicators of social rank,' in Grove in press.

41 Drucker, Heizer, and Squier 1959, fig. 41.

42 See for example Jeffrey Parsons, *Prehistoric Settlement Patterns in the Texcoco Region, Mexico*, Memoirs of the Museum of Anthropology 3, University of Michigan, Ann Arbor (1971), 21–4.

43 Grove in press, chapter 3, note 5.

Chapter 7

44 Elizabeth Wing, 'The use of dogs for food: an adaptation to the coastal environment,' *Prehistoric Coastal Adaptations: The Economy and Ecology of Maritime Middle America*, Academic Press, New York (1978), 29–41.

45 Margaret Schoeninger, *Dietary Reconstruction at Chalcatzingo, a Formative Period Site in Morelos, Mexico*, Technical Reports 9, Contributions in Human Biology 2, Museum of Anthropology, University of Michigan, Ann Arbor, 1979; and 'Diet and status at Chalcatzingo: some empirical and technical aspects of strontium analysis,' *American Journal of Physical Anthropology* 51 (1979), 295–310.

46 Gulf coast examples occur in artifacts from La Venta and Tres Zapotes now at the Smithsonian Institution. Those from Oaxaca have been reported to us by Kent Flannery and Marcus Winter.

47 Kent Flannery and Joyce Marcus, 'Formative Oaxaca and the Zapotec cosmos,' *American Scientist* 64 (1976), 374–83; Nanette Pyne, 'The fire-serpent and were-jaguar in Formative Oaxaca: a contingency table analysis,' in Flannery 1976, 272–80.

48 An analysis of intra-site design variability similar to that conducted in Oaxaca (see note 47 above) is being carried out by the author on the ceramics with double-line-break motifs from Chalcatzingo.

49 Alfonso Velasco, *Geografia y Estadistica de la Republica Mexicana* VII, Secretaria de Fomento, Mexico (1890), 23; Instituto Geologico de Mexico, *Boletin* 40, Secretaria de Industria, Comercio y Trabajo, Mexico (1923), 260.

50 We express our appreciation to Dr Clifford Evans for making the collections available to Ann Cyphers Guillen. See also notes 25 and 46.

51 Southern influences on the Gulf coast have been hypothesized by Arthur Demarest in 'A re-evaluation of the archaeological sequences of Preclassic Chiapas,' *Middle American Research Institute Publication* 22, Tulane University, New Orleans (1976), 75–107.

52 See note 31, Stanley Boggs 1950; Robert Sharer, 'Pottery and conclusions,' *Prehistory of Chalchuapa, El Salvador*, III, University of Pennsylvania Press, Philadelphia (1978), 124–5, figs 11, 14.

53 See note 30, Flannery and Marcus 1976.

54 See note 12, particularly Vaillant 1931, 99–152.

55 See for example Thomas Lee Jr, *The Artifacts of Chiapa de Corzo, Chiapas, Mexico*, Papers of the New World Archaeological Foundation 26, Brigham Young University, Provo (1969), 62–5.

56 Project ceramicist Ann Cyphers Guillen is currently reanalyzing the entire Chalcatzingo figurine sample and computerizing the data with the aim of gaining such information.

57 David Grove and Susan Gillespie, 'Chalcatzingo's portrait figurines and the Cult of the Ruler,' *Archaeology* (in press); Susan Gillespie, 'Distributional analysis of Chalcatzingo figurines,' in Grove in press.

58 C. W. Weiant, *An Introduction to the Ceramics of Tres Zapotes, Veracruz, Mexico*, Bureau of American Ethnology Bulletin 139, Smithsonian Institution, Washington, DC, among others (1943), pl. 50, nos 1, 3, 5.

59 See Charlotte Thomson, 'Chalcatzingo jade and fine stone objects,' in Grove in press.

60 Peter Furst, 'Archaeological evidence for snuffing in prehispanic Mexico,' *Botanical Museum Leaflets* 24, No. 1, Harvard University, Cambridge, 1974.

61 See especially Drucker, Heizer, and Squier 1959, figs 47, 48, 51, pls 41, 42, 47.

62 George Vaillant, *Excavations at Ticoman*, Anthropological Papers 32, Part 2, American Museum of Natural History, New York (1931), 399.

63 Patolli is a game strikingly similar to parcheesi (pachisi) in which markers are moved along a series of squares. It is described by several early Spanish chroniclers and depicted in some conquest-period art. See, for example, note 8, Durán 1971, 302–7, pl. 32.

Chapter 8

64 This idea is based on joint research by Veronica Kann and the present author, and was first presented as a joint paper, 'Olmec monumental art: heartland and frontier,' in a symposium at the annual meeting of the American Anthropological Association in 1980, held in Washington, DC.

65 Guzmán 1934, figs 6b, 7b.

66 See Alfonso Case, 'Zapotec writing and calendar,' *Handbook of Middle American Indians* 3 (1965), 931–47, fig. 15.

67 Jorge Angulo, 'The Chalcatzingo reliefs: an iconographic analysis,' in Grove in press.

68 For example, Coe 1968, 114.

69 Peter Joralemon, *A Study of Olmec Iconography*, Studies in Pre-Columbian Art and Archaeology 7, Dumbarton Oaks Research Library and Collections, Washington, DC (1971), 64.

70 David Grove, 'Olmec felines in highland central Mexico,' *The Cult of the Feline*, Dumbarton Oaks Research Library and Collection, Washington, DC (1972), 157–9.

71 Ibid, 155.

72 See note 67.

73 See, for example, note 67; Michael Coe, 'The Olmec style and its distributions,' *Handbook of Middle American Indians* 3 (1965), 739–74, fig. 49. That these staffs are the same shape as agricultural digging sticks used by some groups in South America was brought to my attention by archaeologist Jeremiah Epstein.

74 Maria Cervantes, 'Dos elementos de uso ritual en el arte Olmeca,' *Anales del Instituto Nacional de Antropologia e Historia* 7, Mexico (1969), 37–51.

Chapter 9

75 See note 28.

76 Drucker 1952; Drucker, Heizer, and Squier 1959.

77 Some minor research has also been conducted elsewhere at La Venta. See, for example, note 80 for Heizer, Graham, and Napton 1968, and Román Piña Chan and Luis Covarrubias, *El Pueblo del Jaguar*, Museo Nacional de Antropologia, Mexico (1964), 16–22. The La Venta data mentioned here derive primarily from Drucker 1952, and Drucker, Heizer, and Squier 1959.

78 Compare note 5, Stirling 1943, 322–3, and Michael Coe 1968, 61–3, with Drucker, Heizer, and Squier 1959, fig. 29.

79 Howel Williams and Robert Heizer, 'Sources of rock used in Olmec monuments,' *Contributions of the University of California Archaeological Research Facility* 1, Berkeley (1965), 1–39.

80 See for example Robert Heizer and Philip Drucker, 'The La Venta fluted pyramid,' *Antiquity* 42, no. 165 (1968), 52–6; Robert Heizer, John Graham, and Lewis

Napton, 'The 1968 investigations at La Venta,' *Contributions of the University of California Archaeological Research Facility* 5 (1968), 127–204.

81 See for example Gareth Lowe, 'The Mixe-Zoque as competing neighbors of the early lowland Maya,' *The Origins of Maya Civilization* (1977), 197–248, fig. 9.4.

82 An excellent catalog and description of colossal heads is found in *Contributions of the University of California Archaeological Research Facility* 4, Berkeley, 1967.

83 See note 35.

84 Ibid; Matthew Stirling, *Stone Monuments of the Rio Chiquito, Veracruz, Mexico*, Anthropological Papers 43, Bureau of American Ethnology Bulletin 157, Smithsonian Institution, Washington, DC (1955), 19–20; see note 73, Coe 1965, 751–2.

85 David Grove, *The Olmec Paintings of Oxtotitlan Cave, Guerrero, Mexico*, Studies in Pre-Columbian Art and Archaeology 6, Dumbarton Oaks Research Library and Collections, Washington, DC, 1970; and *Los Murales de la Cueva de Oxtotitlan, Acatlan, Guerrero*, Serie Investigaciones 23, Instituto Nacional de Antropologia e Historia, Mexico, 1970; also note 35.

86 See note 32, Grove 1981, 66.

87 See Drucker 1952, fig. 49; see note 31, 67.

88 See Drucker, Heizer, and Squier 1959, figs 67, 68.

89 See for example the discussion in Bernal 1969, 49–54.

90 The major publication on that research is Coe and Diehl 1980.

91 Ibid, 127, and Coe 1981, 121–3.

92 Coe 1981, 124–5.

93 Coe and Diehl 1980, 314–15, 361–3; see note 84, Stirling 1955, 13–14, pl. 18.

94 See Grove 1981, 376–8.

95 See Coe and Diehl 1980; and Michael Coe, 'Gift of the river: ecology of the San Lorenzo Olmec,' in Benson 1981, 15–19.

96 See for example William Haviland, 'A new population estimate for Tikal, Guatemala,' *American Antiquity* 34 (1969), 429–33.

97 Coe and Diehl 1980, 126–9, 298; Coe 1981, 139–42.

Chapter 10

98 For example, note 9, Gay 1971, 106–7; note 10, Piña Chan 1955, 26.

99 Guzmán 1934, figs 12, 13.

100 See note 50; note 49, Velasco 1890, 22, 90.

101 See note 49.

102 A. Burghardt, 'A hypothesis about gateway cities,' *Association of American Geographers Annals* 61 (1971), 269–85; Kenneth Hirth, 'Interregional trade and the formation of prehistoric gateway communities,' *American Antiquity* 43 (1978), 35–45.

103 See note 52.

Epilogue

104 See note 21, Hirth 1978.

105 See note 8, Durán 1971, 257.

106 See note 3.

Bibliography

BENSON, Elizabeth (ed.), *The Olmec and Their Neighbors*, Dumbarton Oaks Research Library and Collection, Washington, DC, 1981.

BERNAL, Ignacio, *The Olmec World*, University of California Press, Berkeley and Los Angeles, 1969.

COE, Michael, *America's First Civilization*, American Heritage Publishing Company, New York, 1968.

COE, Michael, 'San Lorenzo Tenochtitlan,' *Handbook of Middle American Indians, Supplement 1*, University of Texas Press, Austin, 1981, 117-46.

COE, Michael and Richard DIEHL, *In the Land of the Olmec*, 2 vols, University of Texas Press, Austin, 1980.

DRUCKER, Philip, *La Venta, Tabasco: A Study of Olmec Ceramics and Art*, Bureau of American Ethnology Bulletin 153, Smithsonian Institution, Washington, DC, 1952.

DRUCKER, Philip, Robert HEIZER, and Robert SQUIER, *Excavations at La Venta, Tabasco, 1955*, Bureau of American Ethnology Bulletin 170, Smithsonian Institution, Washington, DC, 1959.

FLANNERY, Kent (ed.), *The Early Mesoamerican Village*, Academic Press, New York, 1976.

FLANNERY, Kent, Joyce MARCUS, and Stephen KOWALEWSKI, 'The Preceramic and Formative in the Valley of Oaxaca,' *Handbook of Middle American Indians, Supplement 1*, University of Texas Press, Austin, 1981, 48-93.

GROVE, David, 'The highland Olmec manifestation: a consideration of what it is and isn't,' *Mesoamerican Archaeology: New Approaches*, University of Texas Press, Austin, 1974, 109-28.

GROVE, David, 'The Formative Period and the Evolution of Complex Culture,' *Handbook of Middle American Indians, Supplement 1*, University of Texas Press, Austin, 1981, 373-91.

GROVE, David (ed.), *Ancient Chalcatzingo: the People of the Cerros* (in press), University of Texas Press, Austin.

GROVE, David, Kenneth HIRTH, David BUGE, and Ann CYPHERS, 'Formative period settlement and cultural development at Chalcatzingo, Morelos, Mexico,' *Science* 192 (1976), 1203-10.

GUZMÁN, Eulalia, 'Los Relieves de las rocas del Cerro de la Cantera, Jonacatepec, Morelos,' *Anales del Museo Nacional de Arqueologia, Historia e Etnographia 1*, Epoca 5 (1934).

List of illustrations

Color plates

Chalcatzingo Project photos are by Alex Apostolides, Lowell Greenberg, and David Grove. Unacknowledged photos are by the author.

Monochrome plates

Unless otherwise acknowledged, photos are by the Chalcatzingo Project, and were taken by Alex Apostolides, David Buge, Lowell Greenberg, David Grove, Susan Schofield, and other project members.

Figures

Unless otherwise acknowledged, figures are drawn by the author.

Index

Figure numbers appear in **bold** and plates in *italic*.